ANIMALS OF THE BRECKS

MAMMALS, REPTILES & AMPHIBIANS

By **Mike Toms & Stuart Newson**

Published by the British Trust for Ornithology

About the Brecks

As you travel across East Anglia and enter the area known as the Brecks, the look and feel of the landscape changes dramatically. Wide vistas, vast skies and sandy fields divided by rows of twisted pines all confirm a sense that this is a world apart. Also known as Breckland, it covers some 370 square miles of inland Norfolk and Suffolk, extending roughly north to south from Swaffham to Bury St Edmunds, and west to east from Lakenheath to East Harling. Characterised by generally sandy soils with layers of chalk and flint, and by a climate that is among the driest in Britain, the local landscapes have a distinctive quality. Native forest cover was largely cleared by the Neolithic period, some 4,500 years ago, giving way to a largely open steppe-type habitat of heathland and with swathes of inland sand dunes.

Away from the river valleys, the soil was light and nutrient-poor, with agriculture basic and often temporary. Sections of heath were periodically ploughed or broken (hence the term "brecks") and then cropped for a few years before the land was exhausted and the fields allowed to revert to heathland. Sheep husbandry and the rearing of Rabbits in managed warrens proved to be more productive forms of land use, ensuring that the treeless open heaths of the area survived until the early years of the 20th century. Only with the arrival of large-scale commercial timber production (the Forestry Commission began planting Thetford Forest in 1922) and intensive arable farming, made possible by artificial fertilisers and pesticides, did the traditional Brecks landscape begin to change.

Wildlife abounded on the open heaths, which became the last refuge of species driven to the brink of extinction elsewhere in Britain. It was a world described lyrically by W G Clarke – a local amateur archaeologist and natural historian who coined the term "Breckland" – in his many articles and celebrated book, *In Breckland Wilds* (1925). Although the face of the Brecks has changed much since Clarke's day, the area remains rich in wildlife. The forestry plantations have provided a range of new habitat opportunities, and recent heathland restoration schemes have helped improve the fortunes of many of the specialist birds and plants. A biodiversity audit published by the University of East Anglia in 2010 revealed that the area supports some 12,500 species, including 28 per cent of all those considered rare or under threat – more than in any other part of the UK. With several flagship reserves and many other accessible habitats, the Brecks offers some of the best wildlife watching anywhere in the country.

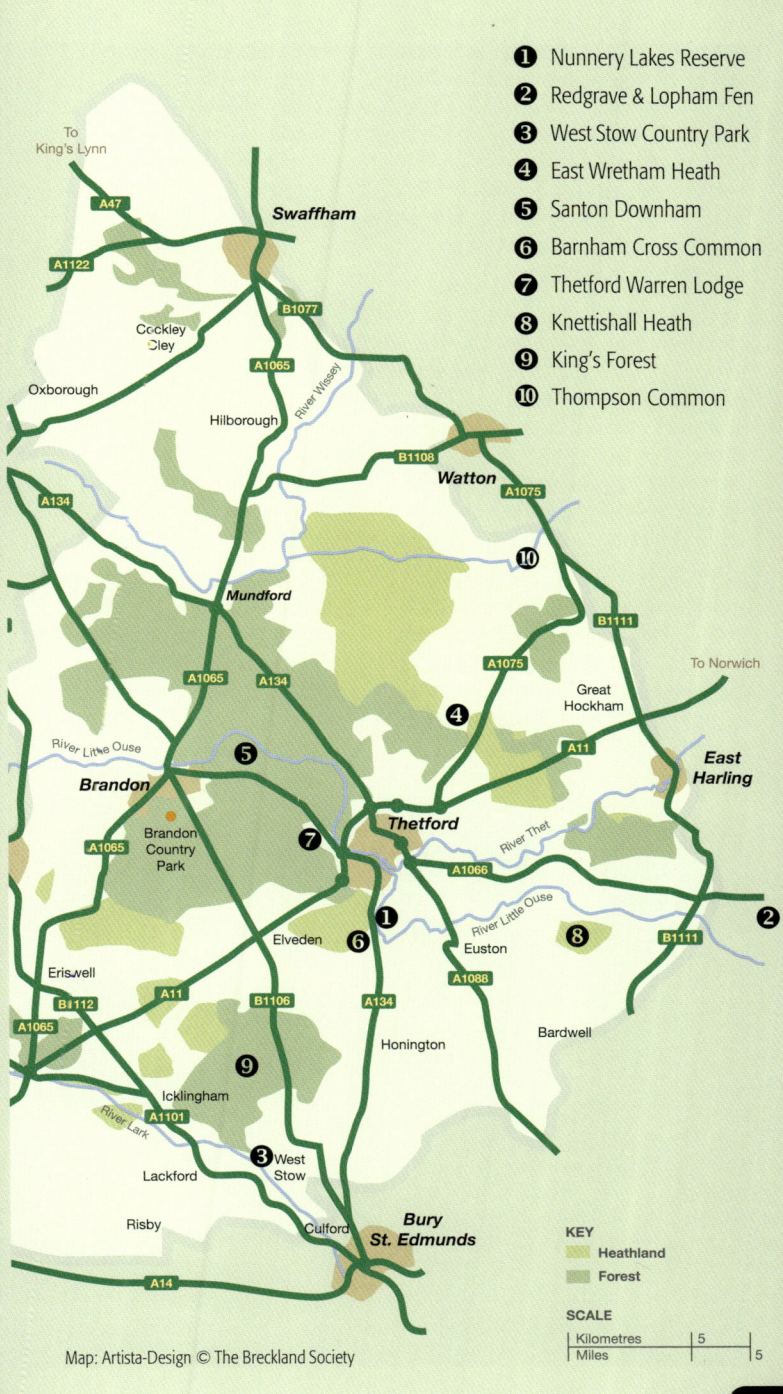

Watching mammals in the Brecks

Although Breckland supports a wide range of mammal species, from the tiny Pygmy Shrew up to the majestic Red Deer, many of these are difficult to see. This is because mammals tend to occur at lower densities than many other types of wildlife and are often secretive in habits and nocturnal in their activity. If you want to see a particular species then you have to understand both its habitat preferences and behaviour, choosing the most appropriate methods and approaches in order to maximise your chances of seeing it. This could involve the use of live-traps to view small mammals, or dawn visits to particular stretches of river for species like Otter.

Bats present a particular challenge, and not just because of their nocturnal habits. Many bat species look superficially similar and require careful examination in the hand if an identification is to be secured. Fortunately, the development of new technologies for recording bat calls and then analysing their structure has greatly increased our ability to identify individual species. This approach has been pioneered by the Norfolk Bat Survey (www.batsurvey.org), which encourages members of the public to borrow an automated bat detector from a participating library or visitor centre so that people can collect information on the bats present at sites across the county.

Larger mammals may be seen at nature reserves, on farmland or in Thetford Forest and other woodland sites. Details of the best sites to visit are highlighted in most of the species accounts, with many of these shown on the map presented at the start of this book. Sometimes it is possible to determine the presence of a mammal species at a site through the field signs that it has left behind. Vocalisations, such as the bark of a Red Fox or the roar of a Red Deer, can also be used for this purpose.

Muntjac, by Paul Newton / BTO

MAMMALS

Making your sightings count – why should I record wildlife?

Being out in the countryside and identifying the mammals that you find is always exciting, but the value of your enjoyment can be greatly enhanced when your sightings are shared with organisations that seek to understand our wildlife. Knowing what mammals are present at a site that you visit is really important, and the building block to knowing how an area can be managed to conserve wildlife. Noting down or recording your sightings as 'biological records' is not only vital for managing our best sites, but it also allows us to protect those sites from the impact of housing and other types of development.

What should you record?

A biological record is simply a note of a species observed by a person at a location on a given date. Records must contain four essential pieces of information:

- What species was observed (either common name or scientific name).
- Where was it observed (ideally a six-figure grid reference or better).
- When was it observed (ideally the exact date).
- Who recorded it (full name of the person who made the sighting).

Who should you send records to?

Norfolk Biodiversity Information Service (NBIS) and Suffolk Biodiversity Information Service (SBIS) are the Local Environmental Records Centres (LERC) covering the Brecks. These organisations are the central point for all records in their respective counties. You may submit your records by using their online systems or you can email the records directly. As you become more interested in recording mammals you may want to send your records direct to the relevant County Recorder, who verifies the records NBIS and SBIS receive. Information on who these people are can be found on the Norfolk and Norwich Naturalists' Society (NNNS) and the Suffolk Naturalists' Society (SNS) websites. If you are recording in more than one part of the country you could record on one platform, the most popular of which is iRecord (both website and mobile phone app are available).

Getting involved in monitoring and surveys

If you are reasonably competent in recording mammals and/or wish to volunteer more regularly you can take part in many monitoring or survey projects. In addition to the Norfolk Bat Survey mentioned on the previous page, there are periodic single species surveys, operated as part of larger national projects.

Learning more

If you are new to mammal watching, or would like to develop your identification skills, the following are good ways to learn and get involved:

- There are many local clubs and societies that will put you in touch with likeminded people, such as the NNNS or SNS (see above).
- The Mammal Society is the national organisation leading the conservation of UK mammals. It has developed a Mammal Mapper mobile phone app, providing information on mammals and enabling you to record them.
- Ispot is a friendly and free online community helping you to identify and share wildlife sightings and is a great place for beginners; find out more at www.ispotnature.org.

Grey Squirrel
Sciurus carolinensis

This non-native species, first introduced to the UK in the 1870s, is now one of our most successful and familiar mammals. It occurs throughout Breckland, occupying those habitats where there is mature tree cover and often pushing into town centre parks and urban gardens. The arrival of the Grey Squirrel has seen the loss of the native Red Squirrel, a species for which Breckland was one of the last southern English strongholds.

Description: Predominantly grey in colour, the Grey Squirrel may show areas of brown fur, particularly on the head, the middle of the back and the flanks. Head and body length averages 26 cm, with the bushy tail adding another 22 cm or so. The underparts are off-white in colour.

Similar species: Size, body shape and colour should make separation from Red Squirrel straightforward. The latter species tends to be more agile, foraging more in the outer branches than is the case with Grey Squirrel. Edible Dormouse, a species not found in Breckland, is more similar to Grey Squirrel in appearance.

Where to look: Occurs in good numbers in areas of deciduous woodland, parkland and the well-wooded parts of our towns and cities. Individuals are readily attracted to food put out for garden birds and may be seen visiting bird tables and hanging feeders. The individuals inhabiting urban parks tend to be the most approachable.

Behaviour: Feeds mostly on plant material and tree seeds, but will also take the eggs and young of nesting birds (though this appears to be an opportunistic behaviour). Seeds and plant material are often taken from the tree, but food is also

MAMMALS

gathered from the ground, a behaviour that is more apparent during the winter months. Surplus food, particularly seeds, is often hidden in caches for later use, helping individuals to make the most of periods when food is abundant and using this seasonal resource to bridge leaner times.

The breeding season may start as early as December in some years, leading some females to produce two litters of 2–5 young, one in spring and another in late summer. These are raised in a nest, often termed a drey, located in a suitable tree. The young first leave the nest at 7 weeks of age, although they will not be weaned until they are 8–10 weeks old.

Squirrels are taken by a range of predators, from Stoat and Red Fox through to Goshawk, the latter a species that now has a sizeable breeding population in the Brecks. Some Grey Squirrel populations are controlled because of the economic damage that they do trees and arable crops. Debarking can be a particular problem in early summer.

Populations in the East of England have been stable since 1996 according to data from the BTO/JNCC/RSPB Breeding Bird Survey, whose volunteers also record information on several common and widespread mammal species. Increasing Grey Squirrel numbers have been linked to the loss of the Red Squirrel from Breckland and more widely across the UK (see below). Despite its non-native status, the Grey Squirrel looks set to remain one of our most approachable and widespread mammal species.

Red Squirrel
Sciurus vulgaris

The disappearance of the Red Squirrel from East Anglia, and its replacement by the Grey Squirrel, has been a comparatively recent event, probably taking place over the period of 1960–1981. Red Squirrel populations held on longest in the conifer plantations of Thetford Forest, underlining that the species was better adapted to this habitat than the introduced Grey Squirrel.

Attempts were made to maintain and bolster Red Squirrel populations in Thetford Forest through a research programme, but this was ultimately unsuccessful. One of the challenges facing coexistence of the two species is the presence of squirrel poxvirus, whose impact on Red Squirrels appears to be mediated by the presence of Grey Squirrels. Although Grey Squirrels are less well adapted to conifer forests, they will utilise them, especially where – as is the case with Thetford Forest – the forest contains stands of mature deciduous trees. Exclusion of Grey Squirrels through control measures might enable Red Squirrel populations to exist within larger blocks of coniferous forest, though this is likely to require significant resources over long periods.

Sarah Kelman / BTO

Bank Vole
Myodes glareolus

Bank Voles occur across the Brecks, favouring woodland and hedgerow habitats where they feed on the leaves of woody plants, fruits and seeds. Populations are influenced by the size of autumn seed crops and so may fluctuate between sites and years.

Description: With small eyes, small ears and a rounded face, voles can be readily separated from mice and shrews. They also sport a relatively short tail – much longer in mice – and less powerful hind-legs.

Adult Bank Voles have warm chestnut upperparts, rich in colour and smooth and glossy in appearance. The flanks, belly and throat are pale silver-grey, leading to clear contrast between the upperparts and underparts. Young animals have grey-brown upperparts with less contrast.

Similar species: Young individuals may be confused with Field Vole, so look at tail length. In Bank Vole the tail is longer relative to the body size, being roughly half the length of the head and body. Bank Vole has a neater appearance than Field Vole because the latter species has longer guard hairs (see opposite).

Where to look: More of a woodland species than Field Vole, occurring in greatest numbers within mixed and deciduous woodland. It can, however, also been found in hedgerows, farmland field margins, gardens and grassland sites. Thick ground cover appears to be important for this species. Individuals are most likely to be encountered through live-trapping projects or as a result of cat predation. Bank Voles are also attracted to bird feeding stations in gardens, taking spilt seed from the ground beneath hanging feeders.

Behaviour: The Bank Vole breeding season runs from March through to October, the first young of the year appearing as early as April. Both sexes maintain breeding territories, with those of the males being the larger in size. The resulting youngsters move away from where they were raised, dispersing through hedgerows and other features with suitable ground cover. During the autumn, individuals may cache seeds, either in the walls of the tunnel systems that these small mammals occupy or under leaf litter. Caches are usually small, each numbering just a dozen or so seeds, but large number of seeds or nuts may sometimes be collected, perhaps even leading to a substantial pile in an outbuilding or shed.

Woodland populations are prey to Tawny Owl and Weasel, with these two predators taking a significant proportion of Bank Vole populations each year. Bank Vole remains may also be recovered from Barn Owl pellets, where identification is possible by looking at the nature of the root pattern evident in the skull and jaws. The UK population is thought to number between 15 and 54 million individuals, but quality information is lacking. Similarly, we have little information on whether the population has increased or decreased over recent decades.

MAMMALS

Field Vole
Microtus agrestis

The Field Vole is a common and widespread species, associated with rough grassland habitats such as those found in young conifer plantations, wet meadows and the margins of arable fields.

Description: As with Bank Vole, the small ears, small eyes and rounded face separate this species from the mice and shrews. Field Voles have a somewhat scruffy appearance, their longer guard hairs giving the fur a less smooth appearance than seen in Bank Vole. While the colour of the fur may vary from brown (with a yellow tinge) to grey, it never shows the deep chestnut coloration of an adult Bank Vole. Although the underparts are paler than the upperparts, there is little contrast evident between the two.

Similar species: Confusion between young Field and Bank Voles is possible if colour alone is considered, so look instead at tail length. In Bank Vole the tail is equivalent to roughly half the head and body length, while in Field Vole it is noticeably shorter (hence the other name sometimes used for this species of 'Short-tailed Vole'). Young Water Voles can look similar to a Field Vole but have relatively longer tails and larger hind-feet (greater than 21 mm in length).

Where to look: Field Voles favour rough grassland habitats, often damp in nature and typically ungrazed. Herbivorous in habits, these voles require a dense sward structure within which they can build their system of runs. Runs may be found by parting the sward and searching; once located, look for grass clippings and droppings to determine occupancy.

Populations may also be found in areas of clearfell plantation, where the bare ground has been succeeded by a well-developed grassy sward. Individuals may be observed through the use of live-traps and may also be encountered as a result of cat predation or in the pellets of Barn Owl, for which Field Vole is typically the favoured prey species.

Behaviour: Evidence from live-trapping suggests that Field Voles are more active at night than during the day, with activity also influenced by weather conditions and time of year. Populations tend to increase from a post-winter trough to a mid-summer peak, though particularly dry summers (with little grass growth) can limit recruitment. In some areas populations may show pronounced cycles in abundance between years, something that appears to be more prominent in northern populations than southern ones.

Although Field Voles can sometimes be a pest of agriculture and forestry, damaging arable crops and forest trees, they are an important prey species for a suite of predators. Loss of rough grassland habitats, across Breckland and more widely, has almost certainly brought about a decline in their population. Nevertheless, there are thought to be 60 million Field Voles in Britain.

Water Vole
Arvicola amphibius

Although not common within the Brecks, this Biodiversity Action Plan species may be seen on some of the local rivers and river valley fens. Once common and widespread, Water Vole populations have declined dramatically since the late 1980s, prompting significant conservation efforts to be directed towards this species.

Description: The largest of our voles, and almost the size of a Common Rat, with a head/body length of 14–22 cm and a tail of 10–14 cm. The fur is dark brown, sometimes black, and the animal has a rounded head, small eyes, small ears and a short tail. The presence of Water Voles at a site may be revealed by their characteristic latrines, where cylindrical, blunt-ended droppings (8–12 mm in length and 3–4 mm in width) are deposited. The more latrines there are at a site the more Water Voles. Feeding remains, in the form of neat piles of grass, sedge or reed clippings, are also worth looking out for. Water Voles make a distinctive 'plop' sound when entering the water, something that is thought to serve as a territorial warning to other individuals.

Similar species: Confusion is possible with Common Rat – a species that will happily take to the water – something that is perhaps increased by the name 'water rat' sometimes applied to the Water Vole. In addition to the differences in colour – Water Vole is darker in colour – the more rounded features of Water Vole, together with its short hairy tail and buoyancy in the water when swimming, all help to separate the two species.

Where to look: The Water Vole may be seen on some of Breckland's local rivers and river valley fens, where its presence may also be revealed by the presence of

MAMMALS

characteristic latrines and piles of plant clippings. The river valley fens at Redgrave & Lopham and Market Weston (both Suffolk Wildlife Trust reserves), together with Blo Norton Fen, have recent records of the species and are well-worth visiting, as are Lakenheath Fen (RSPB) and West Stow Country Park (Suffolk County Council). Animals may also be seen on occasion at The Nunnery Lakes Reserve in Thetford and along the shallow river stretches at Castle Acre to the north of Swaffham; the chalk streams at the latter site proving particularly attractive to the species.

Behaviour: Water Voles occupy burrow systems, excavated into the soft soil of riverside banks where the species occurs along slow-flowing rivers. Populations living away from rivers in freshwater fens and marshes may build their nests above ground in the base of sedges or reeds. Above ground nests are more common where the water table is high, presumably because of the greater risk of flooding.

Populations tend to occur in colonies, with colony size dependent upon population density and food availability. During the breeding season female Water Voles establish individual territories, while the home ranges of the males frequently overlap. Dominant males have larger home ranges and have greater access to the females, resulting in them siring a greater proportion of the young raised within the broader colony. Scent marking appears to be important for asserting social status and there may be combative encounters between individuals on occasion, often accompanied with aggressive chattering of the teeth.

Individuals are more active outside of their burrow systems during the summer months than is the case in winter. Activity appears to be equally distributed throughout the day and night, except in the presence of Common Rats (which are active more at night) when Water Voles shift much of their activity towards the day-time. Populations, which declined during the 1990s, have suffered from changes to river management and predation from introduced American Mink. Mink control and riverbank restoration projects, together with captive breeding and release programmes, have helped the species to recolonise former sites.

John Harding / BTO

Harvest Mouse
Micromys minutus

Our smallest species of mouse is most likely to be encountered in reedbeds, cereal crops and arable margins, where its distinctive cricket-ball-sized nest may sometimes be found. It may also occur in areas of rough grassland and wet fen.

Description: The small size (head/body length 5–7 cm and tail 5–7 cm), small hairy ears and rather blunt face allow the Harvest Mouse to be readily distinguished from our other mice. Adults have russet-brown upperparts and pure white underparts. Young animals are grey-brown in colour when they leave the nest but begin to moult through into their adult coat fairly soon afterwards. The tail has a prehensile tip, supporting the mouse as it clambers around in tall vegetation.

Similar species: The coloration of young Harvest Mice is similar to that of House Mouse but the smaller size of Harvest Mouse should allow identification.

Where to look: Easily overlooked, and so our knowledge of their distribution within the Brecks is far from complete. They almost certainly occur widely across the area, occupying a range of sites with suitable habitat. Any area of tall, dense grassland or reedbed is likely to be used, including those that are highly seasonal in nature – for example, ungrazed meadows and fens that are only cut once or twice late in the year.

This is the only British mouse to build a nest of woven grass leaves well above ground level, the presence of which indicates use of grassy hedgerows, bramble patches, cereal crops and reedbeds for breeding. The nest, which is the size of a cricket ball, is supported by vertical stems but not woven into them. Outside the breeding season Harvest mice make greater use of small mammal runs at ground

MAMMALS

level, which means that they may sometimes be caught in live-traps set for other small mammal species. They may also be taken by domestic cats, something that results in a small number of records reported to the Norfolk and Suffolk County Mammal Recorders each year.

Behaviour It is the Harvest Mouse's small size and prehensile tail that enable it to occupy the 'stalk zone', where it feeds on buds, shoots, flowers and small invertebrates. There is some evidence of territoriality during the breeding season, with breeding nests often spaced fairly regularly across favoured habitats. Activity tends to be focused just after dusk and just before dawn, with the species almost entirely nocturnal during the short summer days. Diurnal activity increases outside the breeding season and peaks during the winter months.

The Harvest Mouse breeding season begins in May and continues through to October, or even later. However, most young are born in August or September and leave the breeding nest to become independent at just a little over two weeks of age. At this stage their mother may begin to construct a new breeding nest ready for her next litter of 4–12 young. Individuals are probably fairly short-lived in the wild, only surviving for a single breeding season; those born late in the year will overwinter to breed the following year. In captivity, individuals have been recorded living to 5 years of age. Harvest Mice are predated by Weasels, Foxes, owls and even Pheasants!

Changes in habitat management and in farming methods have probably had a detrimental effect on Harvest Mouse populations. The change to winter-sown cereals will have resulted in harvesting operations taking place earlier in the breeding season, potentially increasing breeding failure and levels of mortality. The loss of rough grassland and traditional hay meadows is likely to have reduced the availability of favoured habitat. However, overlooked populations in other habitats, such as reedbeds and hedgerow margins, may have helped to buffer some of these impacts.

Paul Sterry / Nature Photographers

Wood Mouse
Apodemus sylvaticus

The Wood Mouse is probably our most familiar small mammal, occurring across a broad range of habitats from farmland fields and woodland through to urban gardens. A good climber, the species may even be encountered feeding from bird tables and hanging bird feeders.

Description: The large ears, large protruding eyes and long tail should immediately indicate that you are looking at a Wood Mouse (most likely) or the closely-related Yellow-necked Mouse (see Similar species and opposite). The upperparts are a warm dark brown, while the underparts are white. Young individuals are grey-brown in colour and may be confused with House Mouse (see Similar species and page 16).

Similar species: Wood Mouse may be confused with the less common Yellow-necked Mouse, a closely-related species that has a more southerly distribution in East Anglia and is usually restricted to mature deciduous woodland and mature hedgerows. Separating the two species requires careful attention. If you get to view an individual at close quarters, perhaps the result of cat predation or through live-trapping, look at the chest. In Wood Mouse there is often a yellow chest spot or streak; while this can sometimes be fairly extensive, it never stretches across the chest to join the brown upperparts on either side. Young Wood Mouse can resemble House Mouse in its coloration; however, Wood Mouse has larger ears and larger feet and lacks the characteristic musky smell of its smaller relative.

Where to look: Although most abundant in woodland, this is an adaptable species and one that occurs in most of Breckland's habitats. Urban populations are thought to be limited by predation pressure from domestic cats but they are still regularly encountered in garden outbuildings and around bird feeding stations. Specimens are commonly found in the pellets of owls and Kestrels.

Behaviour: An opportunist, whose feeding preferences extend across a broad range of animal and plant foods. The foods taken vary with season and availability, with buds, tree seeds and invertebrates of particular importance. Those populations inhabiting the sugar beet fields so evident across parts of the Brecks feed on weed seeds through the summer months, switching to invertebrates – including earthworms – once the harvest has been taken. Young are born throughout the long breeding season, which extends from March to October, with later-born individuals overwintering to breed the following year.

Few adults survive from one breeding season into the next, underlining the high levels of mortality experienced by the species. Wood Mouse is a favoured prey item for woodland Tawny Owls and farmland Barn Owls, with mammalian predators also taking their toll. Populations are thought to be stable overall, perhaps numbering as many as 64 million individuals across Britain.

MAMMALS

Yellow-necked Mouse
Apodemus flavicollis

Thought to be a rare species within Breckland, the Yellow-necked Mouse probably reaches its northern range limit within the Suffolk Brecks. The few Norfolk records come from the east of the county, away from Breckland. Larger and more aggressive than the closely-related Wood Mouse, the Yellow-necked Mouse is thought to be the more dominant of the two. Despite this, it is the smaller species that occurs more widely.

Description: Very similar in appearance to Wood Mouse, this species shares the large ears, large eyes and long tail. Adult Yellow-necks may be as much as 1.5 times the weight of an adult Wood Mouse. They are noticeably more aggressive when handled, vocalising and urinating readily and quick to bite an unwary hand. Although difficult to use as a feature for identification, the tail base in Yellow-necked Mouse is proportionally thicker than that of its smaller relative. The species derives its name from the yellow collar, which forms a consistent band across the chest, a feature also present in juveniles (see Similar species).

Similar species: As noted under the Wood Mouse account, the chest band – which stretches across to the darker upperparts – allows ready separation from Wood Mouse. In juvenile animals this band is grey in coloration. The colour of the upperparts is more intense in Yellow-necked Mouse and the white underparts cleaner, but these features can be difficult to use in practice.

Where to look: The species is most likely to be encountered in the Suffolk Brecks, but even here it is rarely seen. The best chance of seeing one is through live-trapping or by carefully checking the remains of any 'wood' mice brought in by pet cats. The preference for older, mature deciduous woodland and thick hedgerows provides an indication of the sorts of site worth exploring with live-traps. Interestingly, in some parts of their UK range Yellow-necked Mice appear to be more ready to enter human habitation than is the case with Wood Mouse, suggesting that any mice trapped in attics should be checked for the presence of the yellow collar.

Behaviour: Appears to be a fairly arboreal species, ready to exploit feeding opportunities located well above the ground. Their diet is similar to that of Wood Mouse but there is a suggestion that the Yellow-necked Mouse is more of a seed specialist, which might explain why its smaller relative is the more successful of the two in terms of the habitats occupied.

As you might expect, Yellow-necked Mice occupy larger home ranges than those of Wood Mouse, at least within mature woodland habitats. Hedgerow populations occupy smaller home ranges, with overlap between those of different individuals. During the winter months, individuals may gather to form groups.

House Mouse
Mus musculus

Although the House Mouse has a large global range, having been introduced into many different countries, the species has been little studied here in Britain and we know surprisingly little about its distribution or population size. We do know, however, that numbers are largely dependent on human dwellings and their associated food supply.

Description: Dull grey-brown in colour, with smaller ears and eyes, the House Mouse can be readily separated from adults of the two 'wood mice' (though see Similar species for juveniles). House Mouse is strongly associated with human habitation, particularly farm buildings, so a mouse seen away from these is unlikely to be of this species.

Similar species: The features listed above aid separation from adult Wood Mouse and Yellow-necked Mouse. Juveniles of these two species, which are grey-brown in coloration, can be separated on structural features (their larger eyes and ears). The tail of a House Mouse is slightly thicker and more prominently scaly than that of our other mice, something that may increase the potential for confusion with a young Common Rat. The smaller size and different head shape of House Mouse should allow separation from Common Rat.

Where to look: Extremely unlikely to encountered away from farm buildings, such as commercial pig units, or commercial buildings where food is stored. They may be found in flats or houses, though Wood Mouse can also occupy such sites. Other sites worth checking include poultry houses and zoo enclosures (e.g. Banham Zoo).

Behaviour: The House Mouse has a reputation for being a pest of stored foods and agricultural crops, something that has become less of a problem because of the development of more rigorous harvesting and storage practices. They were once common in arable fields, for example associating with corn ricks, but they are rarely encountered in open fields these days.

One reason for the pest status comes from the boom and bust population dynamics of the species, with populations able to expand rapidly when sufficient food and shelter are available. The mean number of young produced per fertile female during her brief (6–12 month) breeding span is 40, and females can become sexually mature at 6 weeks of age, both features underlining the potential for rapid population growth.

Populations here in Britain are likely to have declined following changes in agricultural practices, but long-term monitoring data are missing. Active control of House Mouse populations began in the middle of the last century and it continues today through second generation rodenticides, which are regularly deployed around farm and commercial buildings.

MAMMALS

Common Rat
Rattus norvegicus

Common throughout the Brecks, this large 'small' mammal is readily encountered, perhaps seen visiting garden bird feeders, crossing a road or feeding around benches and litter bins in the area's urban centres. The Common Rat's abundance underlines its adaptability and opportunistic habits.

Description: The large size (head/body length 22–29 cm; tail 17–23 cm), relatively pointed muzzle and long and scaly tail should enable separation from our mice and voles. Adults tend to be grey-brown above and pale grey below, while young animals have a sleeker and more grey appearance. Occasional individuals with dark coloration (melanics) may appear in some Common Rat populations.

Similar species: Young rats can look surprisingly 'mouse-like' but the bulky hind feet, head shape and thicker tail provide useful pointers that it is a Common Rat that you are looking at. Ship or Black Rat, which is now very rare in Britain and Ireland, does not occur in the Brecks.

Where to look: May be encountered running across the road in front of you as you drive around country lanes following the harvest during late summer and autumn. Individuals may be observed at close quarters at some urban sites, notably along Spring Walk in Thetford town centre, where they scavenge food discarded by the town's residents. During the autumn months, individuals may be seen feeding on berries in hedgerow shrubs or around garden feeding stations or Pheasant feeders, providing opportunities for observation.

Behaviour: Probably introduced to Britain during the early 1700s, since when it has spread rapidly to occupy a wide range of sites and habitats. Populations are characterised by colonies made up of several smaller social groups, sometimes referred to as 'clans'. Each clan tends to be centred on a dominant male, accompanied by a number of females and their young.

Where food is abundant, such as in many urban populations, daytime activity is commonly observed; elsewhere Common Rats tend to be nocturnal in their habits, with peaks in activity around dawn and dusk. Predation by Foxes can restrict nocturnal activity somewhat. There is a clear preference for starch-rich and high protein foods but, being omnivorous and opportunistic, Common Rats take a diverse range of items, from meat and fish scraps to weed seeds, invertebrates and even candles. While some items are eaten *in situ*, others may be taken back to the burrow system for consumption.

Common Rats inhabit extensive tunnel systems, often over many generations, and it is within these that breeding nests are constructed. There are estimated to be at least 7 million Common Rats in Britain, perhaps many more. Our knowledge of their populations is relatively poor.

Rabbit

Oryctolagus cuniculus

Breckland was once described as the land of the Rabbit, so common was the species. Its presence here owes much to the vast warrens that were created specifically for rearing this important source of meat and, later, fur. Myxomatosis and Rabbit Haemorrhagic Disease have since decimated Rabbit populations and the animal is now much less common in the Brecks than it once was.

Description: A familiar and distinctive species, smaller in size than Brown Hare and lacking the black ear tips characteristic of the latter species. The coat colour is usually sandy grey-brown, though melanistic individuals occur in some populations. The hind legs are proportionally shorter than those of hare. The white under-tail colour is particularly obvious when an individual is running away (see Similar species).

Similar species: Brown Hare, a common species throughout Breckland, is larger, with longer, black-tipped, ears and proportionally longer hind legs. The under-tail colour in Rabbit is white and this is evident when an individual is running away from you because the tail is held upright; Brown Hare holds its tail down when running, revealing the black upper surface. Rabbits are most often seen close to cover or to their warrens, often in larger groups, while Brown Hares tend to be seen singly or in small numbers further out into arable fields.

Where to look: Although Rabbits can be seen throughout the Brecks in suitable open habitats, such as grassy-heath and pasture, they are best viewed at traditional sites with well-established warrens. These include Norfolk Wildlife Trust's East Wretham Heath and Weeting Heath reserves, as well as Barnham Cross Common, Bodney Camp and Roundham Heath.

Behaviour: The Rabbit is thought to have been introduced to Britain by the Romans or, more likely, the Normans, since when its populations have shaped our landscape – creating short swards and bare ground used by insects and birds such as Stone-curlew – and provided prey for both avian and mammalian predators. Rabbit populations crashed in the 1950s, following the introduction of Myxomatosis, and have been hit more recently by Rabbit Haemorrhagic Disease.

Most Rabbit populations are made up of smaller social units, each largely based on one or more shared burrow systems known as warrens. The character of the warrens is determined by soil type. On loose soils, such as those on Barnham Cross Common, burrows are located where there is some supporting structure from the roots of bushes and shrubs. On more stable soils the warrens may be more expansive, and hold many more animals.

Individuals rarely feed far from cover – typically within 50 m – underlining their vulnerability to predators (for example, Red Fox, Stoat and Buzzard). Rabbits eat a wide range of plants, favouring the more nutritious species of grass, but also taking cereal crops such as winter wheat. In order to secure the nutrients present in grasses, Rabbits produce a faecal pellet that is soft and covered in mucus. This is re-ingested as soon as it has been produced, giving the digestive system a second opportunity to break down the material.

The breeding season effectively extends from February to August, the months during which the young are born, and individual females may produce several litters of 3–7 young. A female may produce in excess of 30 young per year if conditions are favourable (i.e. where there is little competition from other individuals) but the more usual number is 10–20. Young females can breed at 3–5 months of age reinforcing the potential for rapid population growth. It has been estimated that there may be 36 million Rabbits in Britain, with data from the BTO/JNCC/RSPB Breeding Bird Survey indicating that the population declined by 60% between 1996 and 2016.

John Harding / BTO

Brown Hare
Lepus europaeus

Breckland supports a large Brown Hare population, centred on the cultivated farming estates producing wheat, sugar beet and peas. Although primarily nocturnal in habits, individuals are readily observed during the day, especially during late afternoon or early evening. Individuals may also be encountered within woodland and shelterbelts.

Description: This long-limbed, long-eared member of the Lagomorphs, has a more russet appearance than that of a Rabbit. The coat colour may vary with the light and stage of moult, being more russet in winter than is the case in summer. The characteristic ears may be held flat against the back of the head and neck or held erect, depending upon activity. The black ear-tips are not always obvious, in part because of the shadow formed as the ears are flexed.

Similar species: See Rabbit (pages 18–19 for more detail). The other British species of hare do not occur in Breckland.

Where to look: Open arable sites on the farming estates to the north of Thetford Forest, and south of Swaffham, provide some of the best viewing opportunities for this species. Be aware that many of the lanes in this part of the Brecks are narrow and that the wider sections provide passing places for other vehicles. The BTO's Nunnery Lakes Reserve often hosts Brown Hares from the population on the neighbouring farmland, providing good opportunities to view individuals at close quarters. Individuals are easiest to watch when they are using fields that have either been recently ploughed or hold a short grassy sward. Resting hares can be difficult to spot, so it is worth scanning an area carefully and checking over any shapes that initially look like a clod of earth.

MAMMALS

Behaviour: The Brown Hare is an introduced species, probably arriving here during or before Roman times. Unlike its smaller cousin, the Rabbit, the Brown Hare lives its life out in the open, laying up in a shallow scrape known as a 'form' rather than digging a burrow. The depth of the form varies with vegetation cover, being deeper where cover is lacking and just an area of flattened grass if located in taller vegetation. While many forms are located within fields, others are placed in shelterbelts, hedgerows and woodland, with these sites being used to a greater extent during the winter months than is the case during the summer.

Other than those lost to hunting by humans, the main predator of the Brown Hare is the Red Fox, which may take up to 80% of the leverets produced at some English sites. In order to reduce the risk of attracting unwanted attention to her offspring, a female hare (known as a 'doe') leaves her young unattended from soon after they are born, only returning periodically (just once a day) to suckle them. The leverets grow rapidly, beginning to graze from just two weeks of age.

'Boxing hares', which are a feature of the breeding season, typically result from an unreceptive doe standing up to an over-enthusiastic male. The female will first drop her ears in a threatening posture, giving the male the opportunity to retreat. Dominant males guard near-oestrus females from the attentions of less-dominant individuals, something that often involves a degree of chasing and biting.

Grasses and other plants make up the Brown Hare's diet, supplemented by a range of agricultural crops, including young cereals and peas. Individuals may commute between feeding areas to take advantage of particular feeding opportunities, perhaps moving as much as 2 km in the process.

Brown Hare populations declined by 9% over the period 2006–2016, according to data from the BTO/JNCC/RSPB Breeding Bird Survey, which also monitors some mammals. Populations may be shaped by hunting and predation pressure, and by disease – a protozoan disease is a common cause of death in leverets in the UK.

John Harding / BTO

Hedgehog

Erinaceus europaeus

Unmistakable in its appearance, this charismatic animal requires a mix of habitats that provide short-sward grassland for foraging and thicker cover, where individuals can hide up during the daylight hours. Gardens and other areas of urban green space may be used. Populations have declined recently, most likely a consequence of habitat change and increased levels of predation from a recovering Badger population.

Description: This familiar species is our only spiny mammal, being covered in several thousand sharply pointed spines. These are long-lasting and are only replaced on an irregular basis. The relatively small eyes and ears sit behind the prominent snout, at the end of which is a small, dark and rounded nose. The sense of smell is thought to be well developed and individuals may be heard sniffing and snorting as they forage. Males are usually bigger than females, but these differences are masked by variations between individuals in terms of their age, or by seasonal effects.

Similar species: No other UK mammal is likely to be confused with a Hedgehog.

Where to look: Sadly, the presence of Hedgehogs in an area is often first revealed through road casualties. Individuals visiting gardens may be found through the use of a torch-lit search during late evening. Effort targeted towards late April and early May may reveal sexually-active males searching for a mate, but Hedgehogs may also be encountered from late April through into the middle of October.

Hedgehogs range widely, with average seasonal ranges of 32 ha (males) and 10 ha (females), but animals typically travel just a few hundred metres during the course

MAMMALS

of their nightly wanderings. Many follow regularly-used paths and routinely visit favoured feeding areas, which are often centred around areas of damp grassland (including garden lawns and borders). Records submitted to County Mammal Recorders reveal that the species may be encountered throughout the Brecks, though it appears to be less abundant in the west of the area – but this may also reflect a lower density of recording effort.

Visiting Hedgehogs may be overlooked within the garden environment because of their nocturnal habits, but it is worth keeping an eye out for their characteristic droppings. These are long (15–50 mm), cylindrical in shape and dark grey or black in colour, usually with shiny insect remains obvious within them.

Behaviour: Hedgehogs enter hibernation for the winter months; although they make 'wake up' during this period, they usually remain in their winter nest, which is known as a hibernaculum. Hibernation begins in October, with adult males the first to enter torpor and young animals the last. Successful hibernation is influenced by the condition of the individual and by winter conditions. All being well, the first animals will emerge from hibernation in late March or early April.

Hedgehogs feed on invertebrates, with earthworms, beetles and caterpillars dominating the diet. However, they also take a range of other items, and may on occasion take the eggs and small chicks of ground-nesting birds. Some householders put out food for Hedgehogs – and this can provide a way of determining if you have them locally. The best foods to offer are commercially available Hedgehog food, meaty cat or dog food or complete cat biscuits. Do not offer milk, as the only drink that should be provided is water.

Populations are thought to be in long-term decline, something evident from several independent data sets. Habitat change and increased levels of predation are thought to be responsible, though it is worth noting that significant numbers of Hedgehogs are killed annually on roads.

Paul Sterry / Nature Photographers

Mole
Talpa europaea

Although the Mole itself is only rarely seen, the presence of this species is readily revealed by the molehills that result from its subterranean excavations. These may be found across a broad range of habitats, where the soil is deep enough to support them and not waterlogged.

Description: At 12–16 cm in length, the Mole is far smaller than many people imagine. Its cylindrical body, covered with dense velvety fur, supports a subterranean existence. To this can be added the minute eyes, the lack of any obvious ears and the presence of large spade-like forelimbs. The Mole has a short (2–4 cm) tail, also covered in velvety fur. Molehills are readily identified, the piles of loose soil pushed to the surface as a Mole excavates its shallow system of tunnels. These are usually fairly small, about the size of an upturned basin, though they can be significantly larger at sites where the water table sits high within the soil profile.

Similar species: No other UK species is likely to be confused with a Mole, though Water Shrew shows a passing resemblance because of its short dark fur. The nests of some grassland ants can resemble molehills in their appearance, but are typically composed of soil that is finer grained; they also tend to have steeper sides to them and often have some vegetation growing from them.

Where to look: Molehills are most obvious in short-sward grassland and garden lawns, but the species is also present along farmland hedgerows and in woodland. Waterlogged soils are avoided, as are loose sandy soils, the latter because of the difficulty in maintaining tunnel structure. Various urban parks within the Brecks appear to support good populations, as do the BTO grounds in Thetford.

MAMMALS

Behaviour: The burrow systems established by individual Moles are defended against intruders, often aggressively. A single 'nest' is usually located towards the centre of the burrow system and is lined with grass and leaves; females may use more than one 'nest' during the course of the breeding season. From February to May, the period when the females are fertile, territorial males will extend their burrow systems into those of neighbouring females, whose presence appears to be determined through a combination of scent and sound vibrations. During this period the males may not return to their 'nest' for several days at a time.

Litters of 3–4 young are born during late spring, possibly with a second litter following in late summer. Young leave the nest at just over a month of age but do not disperse away from their mother's burrow system immediately. When they do leave they may travel above ground, and it is at this season that individuals are most likely to be seen by human observers. This is also the season when levels of predation peak.

Earthworms are the most important dietary component, but other soil-dwelling invertebrates may also be taken; these include the larvae of beetles and craneflies. Moles may cache excess prey items in stores located within their burrow systems, first incapacitating their prey so that it cannot escape. Such storage occurs throughout the year but appears to be of particular importance during the spring and autumn months. A study estimated that one prey cache of 1,500 g of worms would have been sufficient to last the Mole who cached it for three weeks!

Moles are viewed as a pest in agriculture and of amenity land, often resulting in trapping effort being directed towards them. The use of sonic scaring devices has been shown to be of little or no value in efforts to deter Moles from using an area. Very little is known about the changing status of this species – unsurprisingly, it is poorly monitored – but it is thought that habitat change may have reduced the availability of some favoured habitats while opening up new opportunities elsewhere. Certainly, the Mole appears to be abundant at many sites.

Amy Lewis / BTO

Common Shrew
Sorex araneus

Living up to its name, this is the most common of the three shrew species to be found in Breckland, though it is easily overlooked unless you happen to have a pet Cat or operate live-traps (see below). Common Shrew spends more time underground than the closely related Pygmy Shrew, underlining a degree of separation in their feeding habits.

Description: Shrews can be readily separated from other small mammals by their small size, pointed muzzle, minute eyes and unobtrusive ears. Common Shrew is typically 48–80 mm in body length, with an additional 24–44 mm of tail. The body colour is dark brown across the back, contrasting with pale brown flanks and off-white (sometimes yellow-tinged) underparts. This gives the Common Shrew a tri-coloured appearance. The tail, which is hairy along its length, is paler underneath than it is on its upper surface. Dentition can be useful for identification when dealing with skeletal remains recovered from owl pellets or discarded bottles.

Similar species: Can be difficult to distinguish from its smaller relative, the Pygmy Shrew. Although larger in size, there is a degree of overlap, so it is best to use the combination of coat colour (tri-coloured in Common Shrew, bi-coloured in Pygmy Shrew) and relative tail length. This latter feature is particularly useful if you come across a dead shrew. In Common Shrew the tail represents 50–60% of the head and body length, while in Pygmy Shrew this value is larger, at 65–70%. There is less overlap in body weight than structural size, with Common Shrew weights typically 5–14 g, while those of Pygmy Shrew are 2.4–6.1 g.

Where to look: Occupies most terrestrial habitats where there is good ground cover in which it can forage. Individuals may be caught by pet Cats and brought into the house, providing an opportunity to secure identification from the measurements mentioned above. Live individuals may be taken in live-traps, though note that a General Licence from Natural England is required to do this. The licence permits persons with appropriate knowledge and experience to trap and mark shrews for scientific or education purposes, and anyone using the licence must comply with its terms and conditions.

Behaviour: Common Shrews are opportunistic predators, feeding on a wide range of invertebrate prey, most of which has been shown to be 6–10 mm in body length. Individuals have to find 80–90% of their body weight in food each day, underlining the very high energetic costs that these tiny mammals face. Active throughout the 24-hour cycle, these small insectivores may be heard foraging within the vegetation; their high-pitched buzzing squeaks audible to many human ears. The breeding season, which runs from April through to September, sees each female deliver up to four litters, resulting in immature animals that will overwinter and breed the following year. Adults rarely survive the winter.

Pygmy Shrew
Sorex minutus

Our smallest terrestrial mammal is easily overlooked and very few records of this species are received each year by County Mammal Recorders. The species appears to be distributed across the Brecks, typically favouring damper habitats than those used by its larger relative, the Common Shrew.

Description: At just 2–6 g in weight, this is a tiny species that is rarely seen alive. The fur on the back and flanks is dark brown, merging into the paler, dirty-white, fur of the underparts. The minute eyes and ears, coupled with the pointed muzzle, provide easy recognition that this is a shrew, though identification from Common Shrew is more tricky (see Common Shrew account).

Paul Sterry / Nature Photographers

Similar species: Although structurally smaller than Common Shrew, there is a degree of overlap in both body size and weight between these two species. A key difference can be seen in the length of the tail relative to head and body length (see Common Shrew), with the Pygmy Shrew's tail being proportionally longer and thicker. In fact, it sometimes looks as if the Pygmy Shrew has been given the wrong tail for its body size! The Pygmy Shrew tail is more hairy than that of Common Shrew. Dentition can be useful for identification when dealing with skeletal remains recovered from owl pellets or discarded bottles.

Where to look: Favours habitats with thick ground cover, being more abundant in grassland sites with a well-developed sward structure than in woodland. There is some evidence to suggest that Pygmy Shrews make greater use of damp habitats than Common Shrews. They also spend more time above ground than their larger relative. As with Common Shrew, dead individuals may be delivered by pet Cats or, alternatively, be found dead on paths and tracks during the late summer months (when many adults appear to die off). They may occasionally be caught in live-traps – see Common Shrew for information on the law relating to the trapping of shrews – but their very small size appears to reduce the chances that they will trigger a live-trap and its door mechanism.

Behaviour: Feeding habits are similar to those of Common Shrew, with small invertebrates dominating the diet. Earthworms appear to be taken only rarely, perhaps reflecting the greater amount of time spent foraging above ground, but harvestmen, spiders and woodlice feature throughout the year. Individuals typically overwinter as immatures and do not appear to breed in the year of their birth. Females may have two or more litters, each of 4–6 young.

With bouts of activity throughout the 24-hour cycle, Pygmy Shrews have to spend most of their active time feeding just to cover their energetic costs. We have a poor understanding of their populations, both regionally and at the national level, so it unclear as to whether numbers have increased or decreased over time.

Water Shrew
Neomys fodiens

As suggested by its common name, this enigmatic animal is usually associated with the margins of rivers, streams and other watercourses; however, it can also turn up well away from water in hedgerows, grassland and deciduous woodland. It seems equally at home foraging for food in water and on land.

Description: With a head-and-body length of 67–96 mm and a tail of 45–77 mm, the Water Shrew is larger than the two *Sorex* species found in our area. The upperparts are dark grey and separated from the silvery-grey underparts by a sharp line of demarcation. Many individuals show silvery-white hairs on the ears and some show white hairs around the eyes. The long tail is dark grey above and white below, with an obvious line of stiffer hairs along the underside – these form a stiff keel and may aid with swimming. The large hind feet (15–16 mm in length) also sport stiff fringing hairs, again to help with swimming and foraging in water.

Similar species: Size, coloration and the presence of stiff hairs on the underside of the tail and along the margins of the feet all provide useful features by which Water Shrew can be separated from Common Shrew and Pygmy Shrew.

Where to look: Likely to be present throughout Breckland's river valleys and river valley fens, this species is almost certainly under-recorded. Live individuals are only likely to be encountered through the use of live-traps placed in areas of suitable habitat (though see earlier note about the need for a licence to trap shrews). The remains of dead individuals may be recovered from Barn Owl pellets or as a result of Cat predation. Water Shrews prefer to forage along the banks of fast-flowing streams and rivers, but they will also make use of ponds, lakes, reedbeds and

MAMMALS

drainage ditches, together with areas of fen and wet meadow. Individuals may also be encountered from time to time in other habitats, including deciduous woodland, grassland and hedgerow margins. These are likely to be dispersing juveniles moving away from where they were born.

Behaviour: Water Shrews live a solitary existence. Females maintain individual territories for at least part of the year, while the males appear to be more nomadic in their habits, wandering in search of a potential mate. Although active throughout the 24-hour cycle, peak activity takes place at night and, in particular, just before dawn. As with our other shrews, Water Shrews spend a good part of the day foraging for food, most of which is taken from the water or very close to it.

Aquatic prey, such as freshwater crustaceans and caddis larvae, are brought ashore to be eaten and, occasionally, cached. Interestingly, Water Shrews may tackle prey that are as large or larger than themselves (including amphibians). They appear to be able to immobilise larger prey through the use of a venom produced in their saliva; this affects the nervous and respiratory systems of the prey. A bite can produce a burning sensation and reddening of the skin in humans.

Water Shrews maintain extensive burrow systems close to the water sources along which they forage for prey. These contain 'nests' that are used for sleeping and larger nests that are used by the females for rearing their litter of 3–15 young. Females typically have 1–2 litters and, as with other shrews, most adults die before the calendar year comes to an end; this leaves immature individuals to overwinter and breed the following year.

We know very little about the status of this species, but poor water quality, the drainage of wetland sites and unsuitable management of bankside margins are all likely to have a detrimental impact on populations. The national population has been estimated at c.700,000 individuals, suggesting the species is significantly less common than Breckland's other shrew species.

Andy Sands / Naturepl.

Noctule
Nyctalus noctula

This large, often high-flying species may be seen early in the evening during the late spring and summer months. The broad range of habitats used can bring this bat into urban areas, where it may be viewed from gardens.

Description: This is a large bat (wingspan 33–45 cm) with broad rounded ears and rufous-brown fur.

Similar species: This species looks very similar to its close relative Leisler's Bat, but is significantly larger and paler. Acoustically the calls of the two are similar, although in open habitat Leisler's calls are loudest between about 23 and 27 kHz. In some habitats, such as woodland edge, it may be difficult to separate the two. Serotine is also a potential confusion species, but has a peculiar messy rhythm to its calls, and does not alternate between two call types. Any bat emitting 'chip-chop' calls will be Noctule or Leisler's Bat. However, when foraging within cluttered habitats all three species produce rapid 'chips' and can be difficult to separate.

Where to look: The Noctule is widespread in the Brecks and is found in a wide range of open habitats, including larger towns. The habitats used typically feature sufficient tree cover in the wider area for roosting and a high density of high-flying insects. It mainly roosts in trees, interestingly preferring woodpecker holes over natural cavities, although it also uses splits in trees and rot holes. It can most easily be found foraging over larger waterbodies, and open areas close to or within woodland.

MAMMALS

Behaviour: A fast-flying species, often flying straight across open areas but sometimes diving towards the ground or water to chase insects. There are few studies on the foraging behaviour of the Noctule, although flights of 10 km or more per night from the roost are probably typical. Its food mainly consists of small to medium-sized flies, caddis flies, bugs, beetles and moths. Early in the evening this species may fly high, up to 50 m or more, but it descends to a lower level later in the night. It mainly feeds by pursuing and catching prey in flight and may occasionally forage around streetlights. Common to most species of bat, the females form maternity colonies during the summer months, where they give birth to a single youngster in June or early July. Males usually roost singly or in small groups during the summer. During the main mating period, which extends from July to early September, male Noctules defend individual territories as mating roosts, attracting females by making repeated song-flights.

During the winter, it is thought that this species probably roosts deep in holes within trees, but the hibernation preferences are not well known. On the continent some migrate long distances between summer roosts and hibernation sites, but there is currently no evidence from the UK that Noctule bats migrate. There is considerable uncertainty around estimates of population size.

Calls: Noctule has one of the loudest calls of all British bats. In open habitats it often produces two alternating call types (see below). The first is a call that is loudest at about 19 kHz and the second is loudest at about 24 kHz. As a sequence this sounds like 'chip-chop-chip-chop'. In cluttered habitat, for example when foraging next to a woodland edge, the calls become shorter in duration and extend over a broader frequency range. The calls are then loudest at between 24 and 28 kHz. It may even be possible for people with good hearing to hear a foraging Noctule without using a bat detector!

Bats change the frequency of their calls (in kHz) according to whether they are flying in the open or in high clutter (e.g. flying within woodland or towards a hedge or tree line). The sonogram below shows the extremes for this species, whereas in practice the calls can range and transition between these.

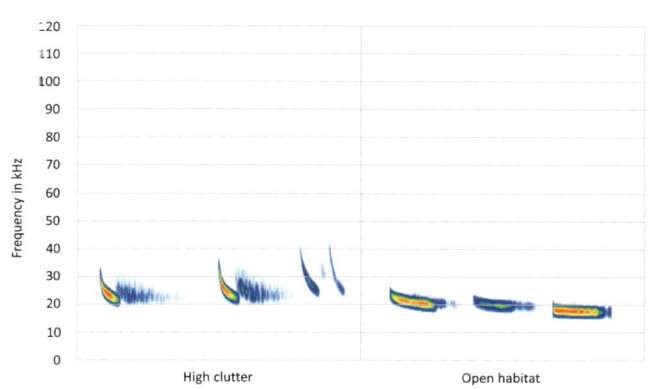

Leisler's Bat
Nyctalus leisleri

Similar to the Noctule, but smaller and with longer fur, particularly around the shoulders and upper back, giving it a lion's mane appearance. It was formerly known as the Hairy-armed Bat. Thetford Forest in the Brecks is thought to be the stronghold for this species in Norfolk and Suffolk.

Description: A medium-sized brown bat (wingspan 28–30 cm). Compared with Noctule it is similar in having large rounded ears and muzzle, but is distinctly smaller and darker than this species.

Similar species: Produces calls which are similar to Noctule, particularly in cluttered habitats where it may be difficult to distinguish the two. Serotine may also be a confusion species, but does not emit alternating 'chip-chop' calls and rarely shows sharp frequency changes of greater than 2 kHz between calls, which is quite common for Leisler's Bat. It is worth noting that Brown Rat, which is a very vocal species, can produce calls at about 21 kHz which look like those of Leisler's Bat!

Where to look: Prior to the start of a bat box project in Thetford Forest in 1975, this species was unknown in the Brecks. Over the years, Leisler's Bats have made regular use of the boxes and in 1998 a breeding colony was discovered in a house in Brandon. With greater recording effort, the distribution of this bat in Norfolk and Suffolk is still believed to be largely restricted to Thetford Forest, where it is commonly observed flying over clearings, and adjacent estates. Brandon Country Park is one of the most reliable places to find this species, but it can also be found on the outskirts of Thetford, particularly to the east of the town, where it can be

MAMMALS

recorded over areas of housing and may occasionally hunt around streetlights. This is one of the few species of bat for which experimental studies have shown there is a preference for foraging close to (mercury-vapour and high-pressure sodium) streetlights rather than in neighbouring dark areas.

Behaviour: Very similar to the Noctule, Leisler's Bat emerges early and often feeds at height, often up to about 70 m. It is fast flying and usually forages in a straight line, with occasional dives and circling to follow prey. Like the Noctule, this species mainly feeds by pursuing and catching insects in flight. Its diet consists of flies, moths, beetles and caddis flies. Summer roosts are often located in buildings but, like Noctule, this species also roosts in natural tree cavities and woodpecker holes; it also makes use of bat boxes in Thetford Forest.

On the continent this species is considered migratory, with long-distance movements being made between maternity and hibernation sites. Molecular evidence suggests that British and Irish populations belong to a separate lineage, where there is no gene flow with the rest of Europe. However, it is not known whether there are long-distance movements within Great Britain, or between Britain and Ireland.

Calls: It produces two loud calls, which like Noctule alternate between two frequencies producing a 'chip-chop-chip-chop' sound. In open habitats the first call is loudest at about 23 kHz and the second is loudest at about 27 kHz. In cluttered habitat, the calls become shorter in duration and broader in frequency. The loudest part of the calls then varies between about 26 and 30 kHz.

Bats change the frequency of their calls (in kHz) according to whether they are flying in the open or in high clutter (e.g. flying within woodland or towards a hedge or tree line). The sonogram below shows the extremes for this species, whereas in practice the calls can range and transition between these.

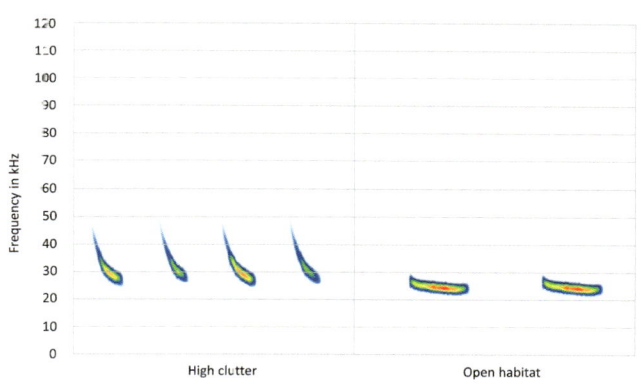

Serotine
Eptesticus serotinus

The Serotine is one of the largest bat species in the Brecks and usually also one of the first to appear in the evening, often emerging in good light. The Brecks is thought to be particularly notable for this species in a wider Norfolk–Suffolk context.

Description: A large robust bat (wingspan 32–38 cm) with a broad muzzle. Its fur is variable in colour, ranging from medium to dark brown; its face is normally dark, and the rounded ears of medium length. The Serotine's broad wings and a leisurely, slow flight, made 5–15 m above the ground with occasional short glides or steep descents, is distinctive.

Similar species: If seen well, normally straightforward to recognise; this is a large bat with long ears, which are typically longer than they are broad. Compared with Leisler's Bat and Noctule, Serotine tends to have an irregular or 'messy' rhythm to its call, and there tends to be more consistency between the calls that make up a sequence. Serotine rarely shows sharp frequency changes greater than 2 kHz between calls, something that is commonly seen in Leisler's Bat.

Where to look: Regularly roosts in rural buildings, usually close to foraging sites characterised by pasture and un-intensive arable. Widely recorded in Thetford Forest, but with peak activity recorded from the villages of Feltwell, Methwold and Northwold, and on Ministry of Defence land at the Stanford Army Training Area. Elsewhere there is evidence that woodland is preferred for foraging early in the season (from May to July), while grassland is preferred from August to October.

MAMMALS

Behaviour: Sometimes observed flying slowly around the tops of trees and circling over open areas, and hunts by aerial hawking. The foraging range of the Serotine is quite large, with radio-tracking studies suggesting an average commute in pastoral areas of about 6.5 km and about 8 km in arable areas. The maximum recorded distance is over 40 km, during which individuals typically follow hedgerows and treelines, and fly over pasture. In spring it feeds mainly on moths and flies, whilst in summer its diet is mainly dung flies and chafers. Most maternity roosts are in residential houses constructed in the late 19th and 20th centuries, which have high gables and large roof voids, or in churches, where access to the roost is usually at or close to the gable apex or the lower eaves. Maternity roosts typically comprise 10–60 individuals and are often shared with other bat species; rarely recorded roosting in trees.

Maternity colonies almost exclusively comprise adult females, with the males roosting separately or in small groups. Radio-tracking suggests that females are faithful to a roost during the breeding season, whilst males use several alternative sites. Despite the Serotine's capacity for strong flight and relatively large nightly commutes, this species is considered sedentary. In south-east England, a large ringing study did not generate any recaptures at a distance of over 10 km. Little is known about the site-level requirements for hibernating Serotines. Few individuals are recorded during the winter at hibernation sites, and it is currently assumed that most individuals remain in roof spaces and cavity walls.

Calls: In open habitats, the calls of Serotine are loudest at about 25 kHz. When foraging within cluttered habitats, the loudest part of the call increases to about 27 kHz and the duration of the calls becomes shorter and broader in frequency.

Bats change the frequency of their calls (in kHz) according to whether they are flying in the open or in high clutter (e.g. flying within woodland or towards a hedge or tree line). The sonogram below shows the extremes for this species, whereas in practice the calls can range and transition between these.

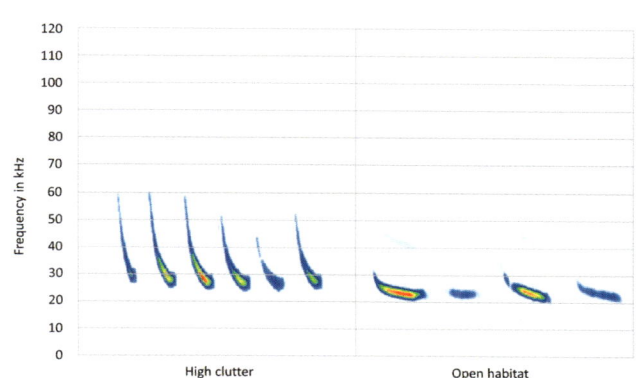

Brown Long-eared Bat
Plecotus auritus

A medium-sized species with long ears, which are nearly as long as its body. Its flight is slow, fluttering and extremely agile in confined spaces. Small prey is taken by gleaning insects off leaves or other vegetation in flight. Breckland is particularly notable for this species in a wider Norfolk–Suffolk context.

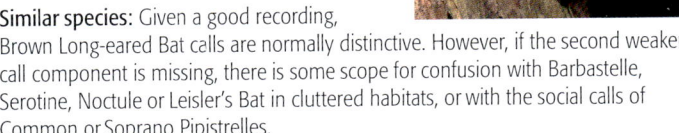

Description: Distinctive among bats in the Brecks in having long delicate ears. Wingspan of 23–29 cm.

Similar species: Given a good recording, Brown Long-eared Bat calls are normally distinctive. However, if the second weaker call component is missing, there is some scope for confusion with Barbastelle, Serotine, Noctule or Leisler's Bat in cluttered habitats, or with the social calls of Common or Soprano Pipistrelles.

Where to look: This species is associated with woodland and is predominantly a tree-dwelling bat, although it will often roost in loft spaces of old houses, barns and churches. It can probably be found in most villages in the Brecks, and is particularly abundant in areas of woodland, including Thetford Forest, where it is the most numerous species of bat recorded in bat boxes. Along with other slow-flying bats, this species shows strong avoidance of light; the presence of streetlights and well-lit areas have a negative impact on this species and its distribution.

Behaviour: Compared with Common and Soprano Pipistrelle, which are most active shortly after sunset, Brown Long-eared bats are much more consistent in their activity over a night. This may reflect the behaviour of this species and the way

in which it 'gleans' (takes) prey directly from foliage and other surfaces which are available throughout the night. The gleaning behaviour of Brown Long-eared bats is aided by an ability to hover, in addition to using slow horizontal flight. Smaller prey is eaten in flight, but larger prey is taken to a perch to be eaten. Regularly used perches can be recognised by accumulations of discarded insect remains, particularly the wings of moths. Whilst moths, particularly noctuids, dominate the diet, flies, grasshoppers and bugs and many non-flying invertebrates, such as spiders and harvestmen, are also taken.

Maternity roosts contain adult males as well as females, although normally with some female bias, and there is a high degree of fidelity to roosts by both sexes. Analyses of Norfolk Bat Survey data has shown that Brown Long-eared bats are reported more widely later in the season, post-breeding. This may be explained by individuals, which at this time of year would include recently volant juveniles, dispersing or foraging further from their roosts and consequently being detected at a greater proportion of sites at this time. This is supported by some limited radio-tracking of this species.

In south-east England, Brown Long-eared bats have shown an increase in mean ranging area in August and September, which corresponded with a decrease in the proportion of time spent foraging in woodlands and greater use of hedgerows. They are generally considered to be non-migratory. In the winter, underground sites including tunnels, caves and ice-houses are used for hibernation, but the extent of tree-use by this species is unclear.

Calls: Acoustically the Brown Long-eared Bat produces calls consisting of two components. The stronger first component starts around 55 kHz and ends about 24 kHz, and the second weaker component starts around 73 kHz and ends about 33 kHz. In fainter recordings, the weaker second component may be missing.

Bats change the frequency of their calls (in kHz) according to whether they are flying in the open or in high clutter (e.g. flying within woodland or towards a hedge or tree line). The sonogram below shows the extremes for this species, whereas in practice the calls can range and transition between these.

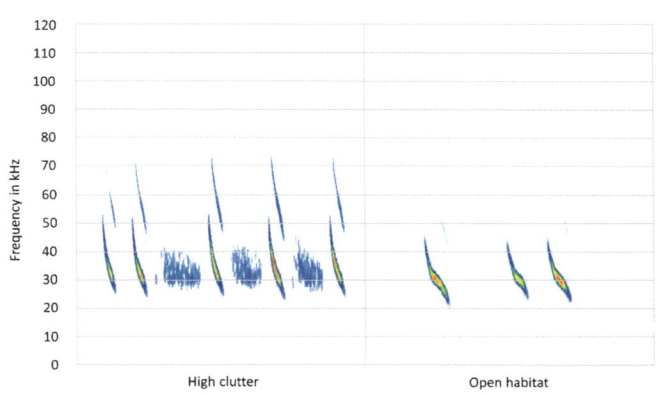

Barbastelle
Barbastella barbastellus

The Barbastelle is nationally rare and restricted in range to parts of southern and central England and Wales. It tends to hunt over a wide area and is a fast, agile flyer and specialist forager in a range of habitats. The Brecks is particularly notable in a wider Norfolk–Suffolk context for this species.

Description: A medium-sized bat with a short muzzle, dark black-brown fur and a distinctive pug-shaped nose. The ears are broad, joined across the head by skin, and covered in gingery-brown fur on the rear surface. The ears project forwards.

Similar species: Barbastelle calls are normally distinctive, but confusion is possible with calls made in cluttered habitats, particularly with those of Brown Long-eared Bat and the *Myotis* species. Although outwardly an unlikely confusion species, Speckled Bush-cricket often produces short calls (between about 26 and 36 kHz), which when reproduced visually as a sonogram may look like those of Barbastelle; however, if played, these bush-cricket calls sound very different from those made by this rare bat.

Where to look: There are several areas within the Brecks where high levels of Barbastelle activity have been recorded, including Stanford Army Training Area. Breckland is a stronghold for this red-listed species in Norfolk and Suffolk, and also likely to be important in a national context. Having a strong association with mature woodland and ancient trees, the greatest threat to the Barbastelle is the loss of mature woodland and older trees with loose bark and crevices.

MAMMALS

Reafforested areas are not suitable for this species, which shows a clear preference for unmanaged woodland. This is used for both roosting and foraging, but unimproved grassland, field margins, riparian vegetation and woodland edge are important components of the foraging environment, probably particularly in the Brecks where the extent of deciduous woodland is quite limited. In Norfolk, most of the woodland found within the Brecks is managed coniferous plantation, with a low density of mature trees. It is interesting that the highest levels of activity recorded through the Norfolk Bat Survey are from private estates bordering Thetford Forest and on the nearby Ministry of Defence land, where woodland management is less intensive.

Behaviour: Between periods of hunting the flight is fast. The species normally forages close to the roost, feeding under the tree canopy early in the evening before then moving out to forage elsewhere, often at considerable distance from the roost. Barbastelle is an aerial pursuit feeder, with a diet that is almost exclusively made up of moths, but it may also glean prey from vegetation. It has evolved a whispering strategy to outwit eared moths, which comprise about 90% of its diet. Moths with ears, a feature that evolved independently in several moth species, can normally hear bat calls and avoid the predators. Some species, such as tiger moths, even use ultrasonic clicks to jam a bat's sonar.

Calls: The Barbastelle often alternates between two call types, which sound like short, hard smacks, in fast and then slower pulses, although either type can be omitted. In open habitat, the first call type is loudest at about 33 kHz and the second call type loudest at about 42 kHz. In clutter, steep calls extend over a broad frequency range from about 50 kHz to about 27 kHz.

Bats change the frequency of their calls (in kHz) according to whether they are flying in the open or in high clutter (e.g. flying within woodland or towards a hedge or tree line). The sonogram below shows the extremes for this species, whereas in practice the calls can range and transition between these.

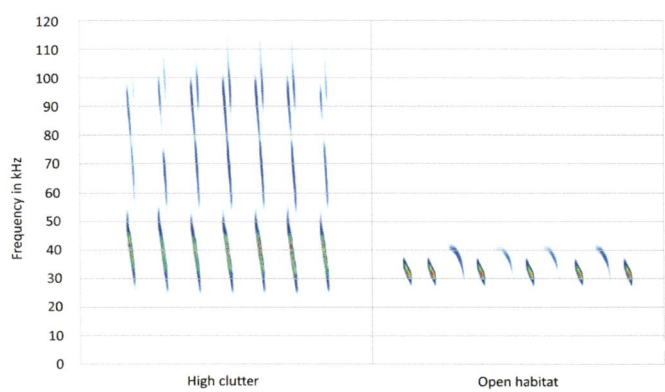

Daubenton's Bat
Myotis daubentonii

A medium-sized bat, and one that is sometimes referred to as 'Water Bat' because of its interesting habit of foraging very close to the surface of lakes and rivers in its search for insects. The steady flight is often made within just a few centimetres of the water's surface. Individuals usually seize insects from close to the water, but have been seen to take prey directly from the water's surface. It appears that they may use their large feet, or even their tail membrane, as a scoop. The Brecks is particularly notable in a wider Norfolk–Suffolk context for this species.

Description: Has short ears and large feet, which are covered with long stiff bristles. The wingspan is typically 24–27 cm.

Similar species: The most likely confusion species within the Brecks is Natterer's Bat, which is similar in size and has long ears. Daubenton's is very similar acoustically to other species of *Myotis* bat, which in the Brecks include Whiskered, Brandt's and Natterer's Bats. The sound identification of these species, particularly in closed habitat, is tricky and not always possible.

Where to look: Strongly associated with lakes, rivers, forest edge and riparian vegetation for foraging and can be found in most areas of the Brecks where these habitats are present. Whilst buildings are occasionally used for roosting, trees situated close to waterbodies or woodland edge are preferred. This species can be found along rivers in larger towns, including Thetford and Brandon, but shows a strong avoidance of areas with streetlights.

MAMMALS

Behaviour: A fast-flying and agile species with a fast wingbeat. It typically hunts very close to water (5–25 cm above its surface), compared with its close relative the Natterer's Bat, which would normally forage much higher. Daubenton's typically chooses to feed where the water surface is smooth, avoiding areas with ripples or surface vegetation such as duckweed. Prey detection using echolocation is more challenging in these areas, but the abundance of flying insects is also higher where the water surface is smooth. Diet largely consists of flies, aphids, lacewings and moths, and small fish are occasionally taken. Maternity roosts are often located in tree holes, but the species also makes use of bat boxes, cracks in bridges and occasionally in buildings.

The life expectancy of Daubenton's Bats is typically over 4 years, but has been recorded up to 30 years. Potential threats include the loss of roosts during work to bridges, tunnels and other structures. In addition, artificial lighting of waterways and bridges is likely to result in a loss of foraging areas and roosts. Because this species is strongly associated with freshwater, measures which influence prey availability, such as water quality and the management of riparian vegetation, may also be important.

Calls: Often produces calls which are sigmoidal in shape, and broad in frequency, sweeping down from about 85 kHz and typically ending about 25 kHz. The start frequency of Daubenton's Bat rarely exceeds 100 kHz. There is often a slight kink or bend in the heel of the call at about 40 kHz. Because this bat often forages close to water, its calls may be missing particular frequencies; this is the result of interference between the reflected call bouncing back from the water's surface and the directly recorded call, something that can produce rather distinctive sonograms.

Bats change the frequency of their calls (in kHz) according to whether they are flying in the open or in high clutter (e.g. flying within woodland or towards a hedge or tree line). The sonogram below shows the extremes for this species, whereas in practice the calls can range and transition between these.

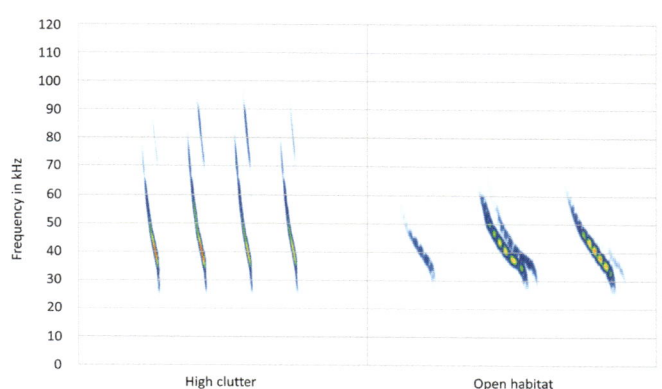

Whiskered Bat / Brandt's Bat
Myotis mystacinus / Myotis brandtii

The two closely related cryptic species, Whiskered and Brandt's Bat, are often treated as a species pair because they are extremely similar acoustically. In some cases they can even be difficult to tell apart in the hand, with analysis of a DNA sample required in order to confirm identification. Both are believed to occur in the Brecks.

Description: These are small bats, smaller than our other members of the *Myotis* genus. Both species have long ears.

Similar species: As noted, the main confusion species in the Brecks are Daubenton's and Natterer's Bats. The calls of Whiskered and Brandt's Bats are very similar to those made by Daubenton's Bat in open habitats.

Where to look: Data from the Norfolk Bat Survey suggests that, treated together, these species are very localised and, where they are found, they occur at low density. More widely in the UK both species are associated with woodland, forest edge, parks, meadows, gardens and water, where deciduous woodland and riparian habitat are selected as core foraging areas. Most records of this species pair from the Norfolk Bat Survey have been from private land with mature wet woodland and parkland associated with some of the larger farm estates in Norfolk and Suffolk, and from Ministry of Defence land within the Stanford Army Training Areas. Both species roost in trees and in buildings, but avoid built-up areas and intensively farmed arable land. Recently, sound recordings have been used to prioritise sites at which mist-netting and radio-tracking can be carried out to ground truth identification and locate roosts.

MAMMALS

Behaviour: Whiskered and Brandt's Bats are both fast-flying and agile species, which forage at a medium height of between 1.5 and 6 m. Of the two, Whiskered Bat is more manoeuvrable in closed habitats, with a fast and fluttering flight. Flies, spiders, moths and lacewings form a major part of the diet of both species. Whilst little is known about these bats in the Brecks, elsewhere maternity roosts are often located in buildings, tree crevices or behind peeling bark, and typically comprise 20–60 individuals. The location of maternity roosts can change frequently, every 10–14 days. In roosts that are occupied for longer, there is a high turnover of individuals.

As with other *Myotis* species, these two bats often visit swarming sites in autumn. Whilst the function of swarming is not understood, it is likely to play an important role in social communication and mating display and is therefore important for the conservation of these species. In Norfolk, hibernation sites include ice-houses and underground tunnels.

Because of the difficulty in distinguishing Whiskered and Brandt's bats, the degree of overlap in the distributions of the species is unknown. More widely in Britain, the distribution of Brandt's Bat appears to be more localised than that of the Whiskered Bat. Currently our expectation is that Whiskered Bat is also the most widespread of the two species in the Brecks.

Calls: Even when treated as a species pair, they can be difficult to tell apart acoustically from their close relatives. The start frequency of Whiskered and Brandt's commonly exceeds 100 kHz and the end frequency is typically greater than 30 kHz. There is sometimes a slight kink in the 'knee' of the call above 35 kHz.

Bats change the frequency of their calls (in kHz) according to whether they are flying in the open or in high clutter (e.g. flying within woodland or towards a hedge or tree line). The sonogram below shows the extremes for this species, whereas in practice the calls can range and transition between these.

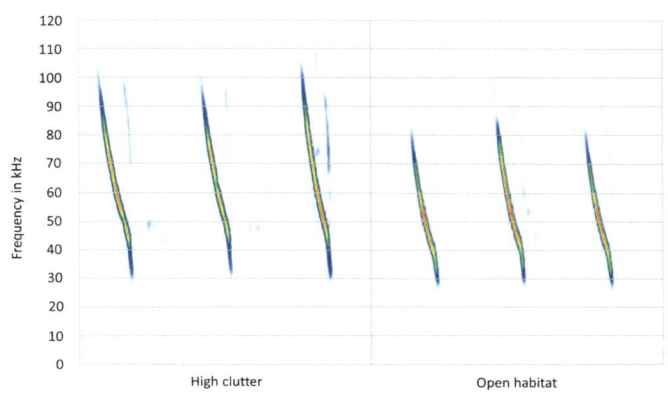

Natterer's Bat
Myotis nattereri

Natterer's bats have a slow to medium-paced flight, sometimes made over water but more often in amongst trees, where their broad wings and tail membrane give them great manoeuvrability at slow speeds. These bats normally fly at heights of less than 5 m, but occasionally individuals may reach heights of 15 m, foraging within the tree canopy. Much of the prey is taken from foliage by gleaning and includes many flightless or day-flying insects, something that provides dietary separation between this and many other bat species. Breckland is particularly notable in a wider Norfolk–Suffolk context for this species.

Description: Natterer's Bat is a medium-sized bat (wingspan 25–30 cm) with long ears and a narrow muzzle.

Similar species: The similarly sized Daubenton's Bat has shorter ears that do not project much further than the end of its nose when bent forward. Acoustically the main confusion species are Whiskered Bat, Brandt's Bat and Daubenton's Bat, which are very similar, but the calls of Natterer's Bat, made in high clutter habitats, are normally distinctive.

Where to look: Natterer's bat is widely recorded across the Brecks. It has a strong association with woodland, including areas within and around Thetford Forest, and still water. Trees are used for roosting, as are old buildings including churches. It is thought that historic churches may support a high proportion of the total Brecks population of Natterer's Bat.

MAMMALS

Behaviour: Flies low (1 to 6 m) to the ground with a slow wingbeat. They are highly manoeuvrable and can change direction quickly. They are unusual in that they forage extremely close to vegetation, often picking prey off surfaces, the prey then eaten in flight. Unlike Brown Long-eared Bat, another gleaning species, moths only form a small proportion of the Natterer's diet. This may reflect different foraging strategies between the two species. The Brown Long-eared Bat detects the fluttering of moth wings using passive listening and relies on sight rather than echolocation at close range to avoid detection by tympanate moths. In contrast, the Natterer's Bat relies entirely on echolocation for foraging.

Radio-tracking work, carried out in Norfolk by researchers from Bristol University, has shown that this species makes use of multiple roost sites within a church, typically located among exposed roof timbers. Whilst Natterer's Bats regularly move between roosts within a church, they are extremely faithful to the church and to core foraging areas. Along with other light-sensitive species, which in the Brecks include Barbastelle, Brown Long-eared Bat and other *Myotis* species, Natterer's Bat will avoid any source of artificial lighting at a local scale. Potential threats include the loss of foraging and roosting sites through conversion of barns and other buildings, habitat change and the use of avermectins, which impact on dung flies – an important prey item for this species. Urban development is also likely to result in a loss of foraging habitat and increased isolation of woodland fragments in the landscape.

Calls: These typically extend over a broader frequency range than those of Daubenton's Bat, Whiskered Bat and Brandt's Bat. The end frequency is often less than 20 kHz, and lower than that of other *Myotis* species. Within cluttered habitats, the calls are typically very short in duration, being straight in shape and extending over an extremely broad frequency range, where typically there can be a 100-kHz change in frequency over 1 ms.

Bats change the frequency of their calls (in kHz) according to whether they are flying in the open or in high clutter (e.g. flying within woodland or towards a hedge or tree line). The sonogram below shows the extremes for this species, whereas in practice the calls can range and transition between these.

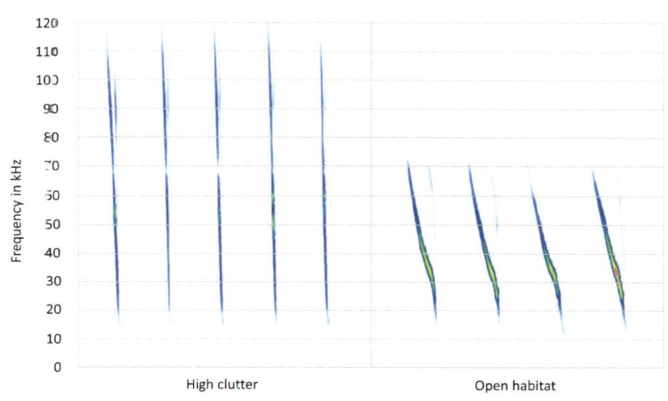

Common Pipistrelle
Pipistrellus pipistrellus

One of the most widespread and widely recorded species of bats in the Brecks. Common and Soprano Pipistrelle look very similar and were only recognised as separate species in the late 1990s. The easiest way to tell them apart is by the frequency of their echolocation calls.

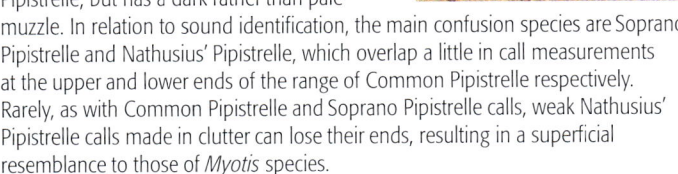

Description: Common Pipistrelle is a small, brown bat with a dark muzzle and short ears.

Similar species: Very similar to Soprano Pipistrelle, but has a dark rather than pale muzzle. In relation to sound identification, the main confusion species are Soprano Pipistrelle and Nathusius' Pipistrelle, which overlap a little in call measurements at the upper and lower ends of the range of Common Pipistrelle respectively. Rarely, as with Common Pipistrelle and Soprano Pipistrelle calls, weak Nathusius' Pipistrelle calls made in clutter can lose their ends, resulting in a superficial resemblance to those of *Myotis* species.

Where to look: A widespread and generalist bat species, which can exploit almost any type of habitat. It mainly roosts in buildings and, along with Soprano Pipistrelle, is often observed feeding around streetlights in urban areas; it is also recorded widely in parks and rural gardens. Although the Common Pipistrelle is considered to be well-adapted for life in the built environment, it is not tolerant to high levels of urbanisation. Compared with the Soprano Pipistrelle, this species is less likely to be recorded in the larger patches of coniferous woodland that make up the bulk of Thetford Forest. It is thought that, within woodland, it prefers to commute and forage along woodland edge, treelines, hedges and forest tracks.

MAMMALS

Behaviour: The flight is fast and agile and individuals frequently change direction. It hunts 3 to 10 m above the ground and catches prey in flight. Common and Soprano Pipistrelles are most active shortly after sunset, which is likely to match the timing of peak availability for small insect prey. There is some evidence that the foraging behaviour of the two species differs, with Common Pipistrelle making more foraging flights of shorter duration. Soprano Pipistrelle spends less time foraging, makes fewer flights, but flies further. Limited information is available on the foraging range of Common Pipistrelle, but most activity appears to occur within 2.5 km of the maternity roost. Much larger home ranges are reported for Soprano Pipistrelle, including from ratio-tracking studies in areas of coniferous plantation in Scotland, where some individuals regularly make flights of over 10 km.

Common Pipistrelle is a generalist feeder, but flies always comprise a major part of its diet. Maternity roosts are often found in houses in crevice-like spaces, usually behind cladding and under any roof covering; each roost typically comprises 50–100 individuals. Whilst the maximum life expectancy of Common Pipistrelle is only 2.2 years, the maximum recorded age is over 16 years. Despite this being one of Britain's most commonly recorded bat species, estimating the size of the local or national population is challenging. The recording of roosts is insufficiently comprehensive to estimate roost density for any part of the country.

Calls: Structurally similar to Soprano Pipistrelle and Nathusius' Pipistrelle. The calls are 'hockey-stick'-shaped and sweep down from about 70 kHz to about 43 kHz, and are loudest at about 46 kHz. In open habitats they become longer, dropping to 43 kHz or lower. In cluttered habitats the call duration is shorter and the frequency higher, with calls loudest at about 48 kHz or more.

Bats change the frequency of their calls (in kHz) according to whether they are flying in the open or in high clutter (e.g. flying within woodland or towards a hedge or tree line).

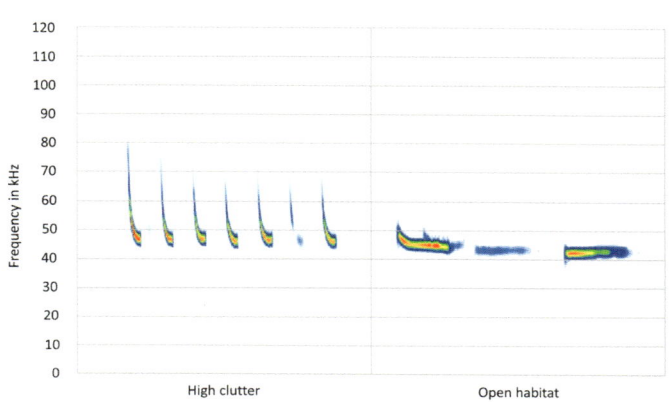

Soprano Pipistrelle
Pipistrellus pygmaeus

The most common species of bat in the Brecks, especially in the large tracts of coniferous woodland that make up Thetford Forest. This is in contrast with the rest of Norfolk and Suffolk, particularly away from water and wetlands, where Common Pipistrelle is most commonly encountered of these two similar bats. In a wider Norfolk–Suffolk context, the Brecks is particularly notable for this species.

Soprano Pipistrelle / John Dixon

Description: A small bat (wingspan 19–23 cm) with a short pale muzzle and short pale ears.

Similar species: In relation to sound identification, the main confusion species is Common Pipistrelle, which overlaps a little in call measurements at the lower end of the range. As noted for the other pipistrelles, occasional weak calls made in cluttered environments can lose their upper and lower ends, resulting in a resemblance to a high frequency *Myotis* call.

Where to look: In contrast to Common Pipistrelle, this bat is much more of a specialist with a strong association with freshwater, particularly rivers and lakes, and with woodland. In built-up environments, Soprano Pipistrelle is more likely to be found in small urban areas and around groups of isolated rural houses, rather than larger towns. Presumably these areas offer good roosting possibilities, with access to woodland and other natural habitats for foraging. In Thetford, for example, high activity is more localised and associated with the Little Ouse River. In the continuous mainly coniferous woodland areas of Thetford Forest, Soprano Pipistrelle outnumbers Common Pipistrelle as the most abundant bat species.

Simon Colmer / Naturepl.com

MAMMALS

Behaviour: Very similar in behaviour to Common Pipistrelle. It has a rapid and agile flight and typically flies 3–10 m above the ground, catching its prey in flight. Both species commonly roost in houses and churches, but they can make use of a wide range of constructions, including barns and warehouses. Soprano Pipistrelle forms large nursery roosts in buildings, which are most likely to be found in areas close to woodland or freshwater, and individuals typically travel further to feeding grounds than is the case with Common Pipistrelle. Maternity roosts are usually substantially larger than those of Common Pipistrelle, and can comprise hundreds of individuals.

Recent radio-tracking work has shown that Soprano Pipistrelle forms 'fission-fusion' societies, with individuals moving with varying frequency within a season between one or two main nursery roosts, each of which supports high numbers of bats, and a large number of alternative roosts. Such roost-switching behaviour makes the monitoring of Common and Soprano Pipistrelle from roost counts particularly challenging and, as a consequence, the Bat Conservation Trust cautions that its long-term trends produced from roost counts collected through the National Bat Monitoring Programme may be unreliable.

Later in the season, during the main mating period from July to early September, males defend individual territories as mating roosts, attracting females by making repeated 'song flights'. The species is considered to be sedentary, although there is some recent evidence from the continent of long-distance movements.

Calls: Structurally similar to both Common Pipistrelle and Nathusius' Pipistrelle. The calls, which are 'hockey-stick'-shaped and sweep down from about 80 kHz to about 53 kHz, are loudest at about 55 kHz. In open habitat, the calls become long, and drop to 52 kHz or lower. In closed habitat, the call duration is shorter, and frequency higher, being loudest at 55 kHz or more.

Bats change the frequency of their calls (in kHz) according to whether they are flying in the open or in high clutter (e.g. flying within woodland or towards a hedge or tree line).

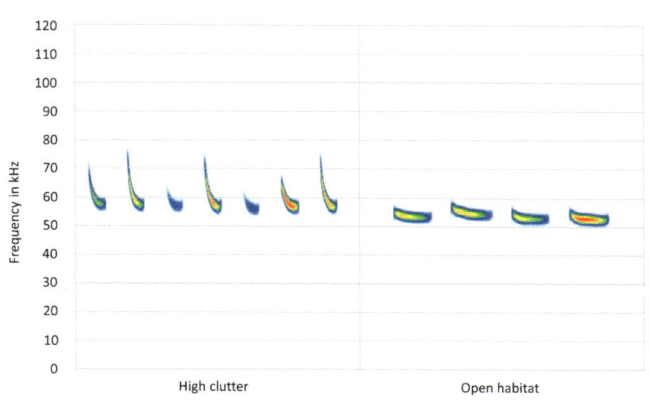

Nathusius' Pipistrelle
Pipistrellus nathusii

A migratory species on mainland Europe and for many years it was assumed that occasional records in East Anglia were only of migrant individuals. With advances in bat detector technology and knowledge of species identification, the number of records in Norfolk and Suffolk has increased, but this remains a scarce species in the Brecks. When recorded, it is normally associated with larger waterbodies.

Description: This bat is similar in appearance to, but slightly larger than, the much more commonly encountered Common Pipistrelle and Soprano Pipistrelle. The fur on its back is longer, sometimes giving the bat a shaggy appearance.

Similar species: Acoustically, the main confusion species is Common Pipistrelle, where in open habitat calls can occasionally fall below 40 kHz and so overlap with Nathusius' Pipistrelle. Weak Nathusius' Pipistrelle calls in closed habitat can lose the end of the call, and superficially look like a *Myotis* species.

Where to look: Strongly associated with large waterbodies, with the Broads being the stronghold of this species in a wider regional context. Several nursery roosts have now been found in the Broads. In addition, the recording of male advertisement calls by the Norfolk Bat Survey at locations across the Broads suggests that the breeding population here may be significant in a national context. In contrast, no male advertisement calls have so far been recorded in the Brecks, with most records of this species from spring or autumn coming from larger waterbodies such as the BTO's Nunnery Lakes Reserve in Thetford. This may suggest some level of movement

MAMMALS

across the county, potentially with additional individuals arriving from the continent, in line with our current knowledge. Recent increases in capture and ringing effort has shown movement of Nathusius' Pipistrelle between south-west England and the Netherlands, and between Latvia and Estonia and south-east England. Some of the distances travelled exceed 1,000 km covered in less than three weeks. In additional, individuals have been recorded in the English Channel by acoustic detectors installed on passenger ferries.

Behaviour: Has a rapid flight and is slightly faster but less manoeuvrable than the smaller Common Pipistrelle and Soprano Pipistrelle. Usually observed 5–15 m above the ground and the bats may be seen to capture prey by aerial hawking. The diet consists exclusively of flying insects, usually non-biting midges, but also mosquitoes and to a lesser degree aphids, caddis flies and other small insects.

The most vocal of the three pipistrelles and, in addition to their echolocation call, they produce very elaborate social calls. The most common type of social calls is emitted by males, delivered from a perch such as a tree or building, particularly in August and September, and which may function in attracting a mate. Whilst we have comparably good information now on the distribution of this species in the Brecks, and more widely in Norfolk, information on the wider distribution of this species in the UK is still poor but improving.

Calls: Nathusius' Pipistrelle produces 'hockey-stick'-shaped calls which are structurally very similar those of its relatives, although typically the frequency is lower, sweeping down from about 51 kHz to about 36 kHz. In open habitat, calls become longer and the loudest part of the call drops to 37 kHz or lower. In clutter, the call duration is shorter, with calls being loudest at about 39 kHz; but they may be up to about 42 kHz.

Bats change the frequency of their calls (in kHz) according to whether they are flying in the open or in high clutter (e.g. flying within woodland or towards a hedge or tree line).

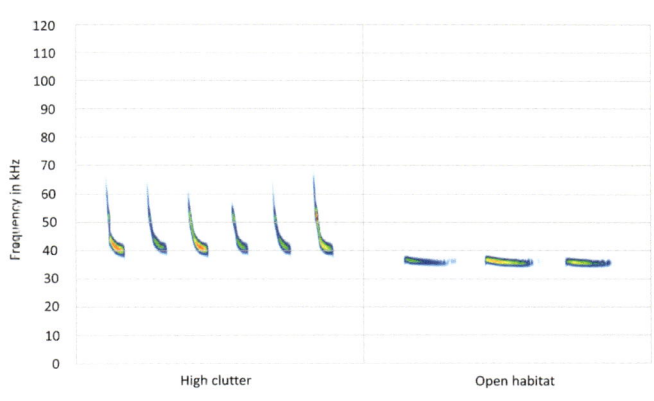

Red Fox
Vulpes vulpes

One of our best-known mammals, found throughout Breckland and more widely across the region. The adaptable nature of this species has seen it colonise some urban areas, though this behaviour is perhaps less apparent in the Brecks than elsewhere. Red Foxes are controlled on many shooting estates, where their presence is viewed as a threat to the Pheasants and partridges released for sport shooting.

Description: Dog-like, with a relatively long and low-slung appearance, the Red Fox should be instantly recognisable. Males are slightly larger than females, but there is considerable overlap between the two sexes. Weight varies with season, as does the nature of the coat, such that individuals have a sleeker appearance in the summer months than during winter.

Coat colour is typically a rich chestnut or yellow-brown, but it can vary between animals. The coat is most richly coloured on the head, back and sides, darkening on the legs and along the tail. The underparts are dirty white in appearance.

Similar species: No other UK mammal resembles a fox in its appearance.

Where to look: Can be seen throughout Breckland, with individuals sometimes encountered crossing forest rides or country roads during early evening or later. Others may visit rural and suburban gardens for food, especially where kitchen scraps are provided on a regular basis. Such visits are often made during early evening, just as dusk is falling, or later into the night, underlining that the Red Fox is usually nocturnal in its behaviour.

MAMMALS

Foxes are most abundant in mixed habitats that offer both cover and a range of foraging opportunities. While large areas of coniferous woodland are used by Foxes, including Thetford Forest, they require sites with good ground cover for foraging and so tend to avoid the larger mature blocks. Hedgerows, shelterbelts and small blocks of woodland provide the types of foraging opportunities that Red Foxes favour and so are worth watching.

Behaviour: Red Fox social structure is based on family groups that maintain a shared territory, the size of which is shaped by habitat, feeding opportunities and the wider abundance of other Foxes. Social structure can vary widely, depending on these different drivers, as can denning behaviour. It is thought that outside of the breeding season most animals probably lie up in dense cover, only using 'earths' – the term for a Fox's den – during periods of bad weather. However, earth use is increased during the breeding season, when a litter of 6–7 young sees the focus shift underground.

With few natural predators, most Red Fox mortality is human-induced, either through direct persecution or as a result of collisions with motor vehicles. While intensive culling can reduce or eliminate populations locally in the short term, the dispersal of young animals from elsewhere soon sees individuals return. Foxes suffer from a number of diseases and parasites, with mange – caused by the mite *Sarcoptes scabiei* – leading to reports of individuals with substantial fur and weight loss, sometimes leading to death.

Data from the BTO/JNCC/RSPB Breeding Bird Survey show that Red Fox populations have declined in central-southern England and Wales since 1995. There is no evidence of decline within the Brecks, though the levels of abundance seen here do appear to be lower than those elsewhere within Norfolk or Suffolk. This may be linked to habitat availability and the potential unsuitability of the large blocks of mature conifers that dominate Thetford Forest.

Badger
Meles meles

Although related to our other mustelids (Stoat, Weasel, Otter, etc.), the Badger is a very different looking animal, with a heavy-bodied and powerful appearance. The white head, with bold dark stripes running up the snout and through the eyes to the ears, should make this species instantly recognisable.

Description: This powerfully built mammal, with its stocky wedge-shaped body, short tail and surprisingly small head, is 67–70 cm in length (head-and-body), making it about the same size as a Red Fox (minus the tail). The overall appearance is of a dirty grey-coloured animal, paler on the sides than it is across the shoulders and legs. The grey appearance is a result of the characteristic colouring of individual guard hairs, which are light at their base and tip but darker in the middle. These may sometimes be found caught on barbed wire, where a regular Badger trail cuts under a fence.

In addition to hair caught on fences and footprints (five toes and a broad main pad), there are other fieldsigns that can be used to determine the presence of Badgers in the local area. Territories are marked by shared latrines, which are shallow pits, left uncovered and holding faeces that are usually markedly looser than those of a domestic dog. Badger setts vary in size, typically with 3–9 entrance holes visible. The holes are invariably at least 25 cm in diameter (often much bigger). Large spoil heaps, comprised of old bedding, may be found nearby and provide evidence that a sett has been in recent use. Badgers may use trees near to the sett for scratching, the tree's bark sometimes marked not just by the claws but also covered with mud from the Badger's fur.

MAMMALS

Similar species: No other UK species resembles a Badger.

Where to look: West Norfolk, including the Norfolk Brecks, is thought to be the stronghold for the species within the county. In Suffolk, Badger numbers are at their greatest within the southern part of the county, but the Suffolk Brecks do appear to be important when considered alongside the rest of northern Suffolk. Published information on the distribution of Badgers tends to be restricted by concerns about illegal persecution, with most records relating to animals killed through collision with motor traffic. Having said that, Thetford Forest supports a number of active Badger setts and animals may occasionally be seen in the forest or crossing minor roads in the area.

Badgers favour well-drained soils for the placement of their setts and require a mix of woodland cover and hedgerows, coupled with earthworm-rich pastures for foraging. Since cattle farming tends to produce ideal foraging conditions, fields with cattle (and to a certain degree other livestock) are worth watching. However, there are few cattle farmers within the Brecks and Badger densities here will certainly be far lower than they are in other parts of Britain.

Behaviour: Scent is an important component of Badger society and Badgers have an excellent sense of smell. This means that they will quickly identify the presence of a human observer if that observer is upwind of them. Individuals may be active during the daylight hours in some secluded sites, but most are crepuscular (active at dawn and dusk) or nocturnal in habits. Activity levels outside the sett are reduced during the winter months.

Badger populations have been recovering from past persecution and the numbers present in Norfolk are thought to have been increasing for some time now. Although this remains a difficult species to observe within Breckland, the increasing numbers will almost certainly improve your chances of catching up with one of our most charismatic mammals.

John Harding / BTO

Otter
Lutra lutra

The return of the Otter to the Brecks owes much to the efforts of those involved in breeding and release projects. Although Otters are typically shy and retiring, there have been periods where particular individuals have been readily observed, most notably along Spring Walk in Thetford from the BTO's Nunnery Lakes Reserve right into the centre of the town.

Description: This large, mostly aquatic carnivore has a broad head and a long, tapering tail. The fur is dark brown, but it can appear almost black in some lights when wet. Many individuals sport white on their upper lip (see smaller image) and/or chin. The head is flat, the eyes and ears surprisingly small, and the animal has long and obvious whiskers, which are pale in colour.

The presence of Otters on a stretch of river may be revealed by their spraints (faeces) which tend to be deposited at prominent sites, such as large rocks and under trees. This underlines the role that these play in communication, with individual Otters advertising their presence (and saying something about themselves) through their scent. To the human nose an Otter spraint has a not unpleasant and rather sweet-smelling musky odour (contrast the faeces of American Mink).

Given a suitable muddy substrate, clear footprints may be found on occasion; these show five toes arching around a central pad (though only rarely revealing the claws or the webbing between the toes). Prey remains, including partially eaten fish, may sometimes be found but are difficult to distinguish from those left by other predators, including mink.

MAMMALS

Similar species: The most likely confusion species is American Mink, although a glimpsed Polecat may sometimes cause confusion; both species are noticeably smaller than an adult Otter. Only American Mink is likely to be seen in the water, where it has a much more buoyant action than that of an Otter, the latter tending to swim low in the water and often with just the head showing (see photograph).

Where to look: Otters are known from all four of the main rivers flowing through the Brecks (see map on pages 2–3) but are most readily seen on the River Thet and the River Little Ouse. As noted, Spring Walk in Thetford has proved a reliable site in the past, though sightings have fallen somewhat over the last few years. Another site that has attracted significant interest is along the Little Ouse at Santon Downham (including the stretch near St Helen's car park).

The presence of an Otter can sometimes be determined by watching the behaviour of the local ducks and geese, which often spot an individual before a human observer does. Otters moving along a section of river often work the margins when hunting, but may move at speed when they are merely passing through. Look for unexpected ripples and bubbles, both of which may indicate that an Otter is present on a section of river.

Behaviour: Breckland's Otters are thought to be largely nocturnal in their habits, but daytime sightings have been fairly regular over recent years, underlining the increasing Otter population now thought to be present locally. The solitary males may range several kilometres over the course of a night, emphasising their presence through their sprainting sites.

As elsewhere, the local Otters are vulnerable to road traffic, especially where they are forced to cross roads that pass over or near rivers. Individuals can range widely, however, including the animal that was caught on CCTV cameras in the centre of Swaffham one evening.

Neil Calbrade / BTO

Stoat
Mustela erminea

A fierce predator, often tackling prey much larger than itself. Individuals are most likely to be encountered through chance, perhaps seen crossing a road, path or forest ride, or observed working a hedgerow or Rabbit warren for prey.

Description: Typically 20–30 cm in body length, with a long (5–6 cm) black-tipped tail, the Stoat has a long, thin body carried on short legs. Within Breckland populations the upperparts are usually sandy-brown in colour throughout the year. While individuals living in northern England and Scotland moult through into a white coat (known as 'ermine') during the winter months, it is rare to see a Stoat in ermine this far south (though it can happen). The summer coat shows pale, creamy-white underparts, and is divided from the brown upperparts along the sides by a straight line (see Similar species).

Stoat droppings, known as scats, are thin and twisted. Typically 4–8 cm in length, they often have twists of fur at each end. However, although intermediate in size between those produced by Weasel and Polecat, they cannot be reliably separated except through the use of genetic methods.

Similar species: Weasel is the species with which a Stoat is most likely to be confused, even though the former is noticeably smaller (head/body length of 17–25 cm and tail of 3–6 cm). Weasel tends to have darker upperparts and the line separating these from the pale underparts is uneven, as opposed to being straight. A Weasel seen running across a road or path has the appearance of a vole or mouse that has been stretched, rather than something bigger.

MAMMALS

Where to look: Can be found throughout Breckland, wherever there is suitable habitat providing prey and cover. Woodland edge and farmland habitats are favoured, with urban sites avoided. Individuals prefer to use hedgerows, ditches and low cover when moving about, and avoid crossing large areas of open ground. Activity is concentrated towards areas with good densities of favoured prey; active Rabbit warrens, such as those at Weeting, East Wretham Heath and Barnham Cross Common, are well worth watching for Stoats.

Behaviour: Territorial in behaviour, with each male territory likely to encompass several smaller female territories. Individuals defend their territory against other Stoats of their sex. Female Stoats are sexually mature at just 2–3 weeks of age, while they are still blind and helpless, and may be mated by adult males. Implantation of the fertilised egg is delayed by up to 10 months, meaning that the young resulting from such early matings will not be born until the following spring. Young Stoats remain with their mother until they are three months of age.

Males – the larger sex – take a greater proportion of Rabbit prey in their diet, while females tend to take more small mammals, such as mice and voles. Rabbits have certainly been important to the Stoat and declines in their abundance following Myxomatosis and Rabbit Haemorrhagic Disease are likely to have impacted on Stoat populations. Diet tends to vary seasonally depending upon availability, with Rabbits important in spring, small mammals in late autumn and winter and with gamebirds, grassland-breeding waders, their eggs and chicks also taken when and where available.

The UK population is thought to number 430,000 individuals but we lack reliable information on both population size and population trend. Numbers fluctuate in response to food availability but may also be subject to the levels of trapping and killing directed towards them by those involved in the management of gamebirds.

Weasel
Mustela nivalis

This tiny predator is our smallest carnivore, measuring just 17–25 cm (head/body length) with a tail of 3–6 cm. It is most likely to be encountered by chance, seen rushing across a footpath or road. Very occasionally, a Weasel may be caught in a live-trap set for mice and voles. Inquisitive in habits, an individual can sometimes be attracted to the sound made by sucking the back of your hand, which imitates the call made by a Rabbit in distress.

Description: Resembles an elongated mouse or vole, with short legs and a long, thin body. The upperparts are often sandy-brown in colour, perhaps a little darker than the colour seen on Stoat (though this can vary between individuals and with the light conditions under which the observation is made). The relatively short tail (about 18% of body length) lacks the black tip seen in its larger relative.

Similar species: Noticeably smaller than a Stoat, the Weasel can also be separated by the lack of a black tip to the tail and by the irregular line formed on the side where the brown upperparts meet the off-white underparts. Unlike some Stoats, Weasels never develop a white winter coat.

Where to look: Occupies a range of habitats within Breckland, especially favouring farmland hedgerows and woodland. It may use both deciduous and coniferous woodland, with parts of the latter used where there are suitable densities of favoured small mammal prey. Individuals may occasionally visit rural gardens but suburban and urban landscapes are avoided. Despite being common and widely distributed across Breckland, Weasels are difficult to find and most encounters

MAMMALS

are made by chance. Where a Weasel is seen to run across a path ahead of you it may sometimes be possible to call it out by imitating the distress call of an injured Rabbit. This underlines their curiosity, something that may also make them susceptible to the gun of a gamekeeper.

Behaviour: Although most active during the day, activity may be shaped by food availability. This is a small mammal specialist, feeding predominantly on mice and voles. However, young Rabbits, birds and eggs also feature when available. In those years when small mammals are less abundant, birds and their eggs may become more important, with individual Weasels raiding nest boxes and open nests for their contents.

Being so small makes the Weasel vulnerable to larger predators, including Red Fox and various birds of prey. It is for this reason that it tends to forage within cover. The small body size enables it to enter the tunnel systems used by mice and voles, a behaviour that is seen more often in females than males. Weasels will also work woodpiles, dry stone walls and other structures that might harbour favoured prey. Surplus prey may be cached for future use.

Males and females maintain individual territories, with those of the male larger in size. During the spring months, males range more widely in the search of mating opportunities. In contrast to Stoat, female Weasels do not become sexually mature until they are 3–4 months of age (the same as for males); implantation of the fertilised egg is not delayed, so pregnant females may be encountered at any time between March and September.

Like Stoat, the Weasel is considered a threat to gamebirds and its populations are regularly controlled by keepers. National populations are thought to number c.450,000 but there is substantial uncertainty around this figure and also around overall population trends. Habitat loss, levels of persecution and changes in food availability may all shape Weasel populations.

Laurie Campbell / Nature Photographers

Polecat
Mustela putorius

A recent recolonist in Breckland, its return made possible by a significant increase in range following reductions in the levels of persecution directed towards the species. Secretive in habits, and predominantly nocturnal in behaviour, the Polecat is rarely seen. Individuals may sometimes be found dead on Breckland's roads, the result of collision with motor traffic.

Description: Similar in size to a Mink, so smaller than an Otter but noticeably larger than a Stoat, the Polecat is dark in its overall appearance, with creamy-white markings on the face and chin. The body colour is made up of grey-buff underfur and darker guard hairs, which tend towards a dark purple-black coloration. This gives the animal a somewhat patchy appearance as it moves. The relatively short tail tends towards bushy in its appearance.

Similar species: The two potential confusion species are American Mink and Feral Ferret. The coat colour – which is uniform in American Mink and mixed in Polecat – and the pale facial markings of Polecat should be sufficient to separate it from American Mink. Separation from Ferret is more difficult and may sometimes prove impossible in the field. In general, Ferret tends to be paler in colour, with greater variability in its markings and a larger creamy-white throat patch (greater than 50 mm in length) than that seen in Polecat. Ferrets often have one or more white feet (none in Polecat) and the dark fur on the face does not reach the nose. It should be noted that hybrids between Polecats and Ferrets may be particularly challenging to identify. If you find a dead individual, take notes and/or photographs of these key features.

MAMMALS

Where to look: The chances of seeing a live Polecat in Breckland are currently low, but as the species becomes better established they will increase. Individuals are most likely to be encountered as a victim of a road traffic collision, and records of such animals should definitely be shared with the County Mammal Recorder. There is a preference for woodland edge, farmland hedgerows and the wet margins associated with river corridors, wetlands and ditches. Agricultural buildings may be visited throughout the year, though greater use of these is made during the autumn and winter months, the Polecats presumably attracted by the presence of rats and mice.

Behaviour: Polecat populations were probably at their low point immediately prior to World War One, the species only present in Herefordshire, Shropshire and across central Wales. Persecution – the species was targeted to protect commercial Rabbit and game-rearing interests – increased substantially from then onwards and the species has gradually expanded in its range, reoccupying former haunts. The present distribution is now at least double that evident during the 1980s.

Activity is linked to prey availability, with individuals typically only spending 3–4 hours each day foraging. Females increase their levels of activity when they have dependent young to fed, while males expand their activity during early spring, when searching for a mate. Diet is highly varied but mainly comprises mammal prey, with Rabbit and Common Rat seemingly of particular importance. In addition to other small mammals, Polecats will also take small birds, eggs, fish and even earthworms. Excess prey may be cached for later use.

The UK population probably exceeds 80,000 individuals, with an upward trend and continued expansion in range. Numbers may be subject to the availability of favoured foods, with any decline in Rabbit numbers likely to have some effect. The species may also be exposed to environmental contaminants in the form of rodenticides used to control populations of Common Rat.

Edwin Giesbers / Naturepl.com

Ferret
Mustela furo

The domestic Ferret continues to be a popular pet with some enthusiasts, resulting in relatively small numbers escaping into the wild each year. Originally domesticated from the Polecat, some feral individuals can look very similar to their wild counterpart. Regular reports of Ferrets from parts of the Brecks were once easy to attribute to this animal but a recovering Polecat population now means that more care needs to be given when attempting an identification.

Description: As noted previously, many individuals can appear similar to Polecat in their appearance, but others may be of the albino form, popular in captivity. Escaped individuals are likely to be much more tolerant of humans than Polecats are, a feature that can aid identification.

Similar species: See Polecat account for review of the main differences between these two animals, though note that not all individuals can be identified on the basis of their appearance.

Where to look: Ferrets are most likely to be encountered as road casualties, but live individuals are occasionally reported crossing roads or visiting domestic gardens, including those with chickens or other fowl. Individuals were sometimes seen around East Wretham Heath to the north-east of Thetford, perhaps the result of local interest in the species or perhaps attracted by the sizeable Rabbit population. As noted earlier, Breckland's Rabbit populations have changed following the emergence of disease, with substantial declines in some areas; the extent to which this might have impacted on the numbers of Ferrets being used to hunt Rabbits is unclear, but the suspicion is that fewer people now hunt Rabbits with Ferrets than they once did. Most of those encountered are likely to be the result of escapes from captivity, rather than the result of a feral population.

Behaviour: Ferrets have been domesticated for at least 2,000 years, with several Greek and Roman writers referring to their use for bolting Rabbits from their burrow systems. Very large numbers were imported into Britain, via London, in the 1880s and again used for flushing Rabbits. There is a suggestion that the use of Ferrets in this manner benefits from hybridising domesticated individuals with wild Polecats. The resulting animals are more aggressive – and more difficult to handle in captivity – but are more effective when hunting Rabbits. Because of this they are also more likely to be abandoned or to escape during hunting activities.

There has been relatively little work studying Ferrets in the wild in the UK, but there is information on diet, reproductive condition and coat characteristics, all the result of individuals killed through collision with motor traffic. Ground-nesting birds, Rabbits and small mammals appear to be the main prey items taken, but larger invertebrates also feature.

MAMMALS

American Mink
Neovison vison

Originally imported for its fur and kept in fur farms, the American Mink became something of a conservation challenge as escaped individuals began to establish feral populations. Mink numbers have declined over recent years, a result of targeted trapping efforts and competition from a recovering Otter population. Although still present within Breckland, they are rarely encountered.

Description: With a head/body length of 32–45 cm, plus tail of 14–22 cm, the American Mink is noticeably smaller than an Otter. The fur is dark brown, sometimes almost black in appearance, with a white patch (of varying size) present under the chin. Although many different colour forms were kept in fur farms, most individuals present today are of the wild type described above.

Similar species: As noted in the Otter account, American Mink swims with a very buoyant action, with much of the back held above the water surface, while Otter holds its body low within the water. When seen on land, look for the bushy tail, rather than the long, smoothly cylindrical tail of an Otter. Like Otters, American Mink use scent cues to inform other individuals of their presence and identity. However, unlike Otter spraints, the droppings produced by American Mink are decidedly unpleasant when fresh. They may be differentiated from the droppings of Stoat, Polecat and Polecat/Ferret by the presence of fish bones and other aquatic creatures.

Where to look: Mink forage across both aquatic and terrestrial habitats, but are most often associated with waterbodies of some form. Largely nocturnal in habits they are rarely seen and your best chance of catching up with one is to spend time in riverine habitats around dusk. As with many of our mammal species, the use of camera traps can sometimes reveal the presence of a Mink at a site.

Behaviour: An opportunist predator that will take a wide range of invertebrate and vertebrate prey, the latter including fish, birds and other mammals. Coot, Moorhen and various species of duck may be taken, with Rabbit perhaps the most common prey away from rivers and lakes. It is this broad diet that has brought the species into conflict with fisheries managers and those working in conservation. The arrival of American Mink has been linked to the loss of Water Voles from some sites.

The breeding season appears to be centred on a brief four-week window in late March and early April, resulting in litters of 4–6 young. American Mink may delay implantation of the embryo for several weeks, which means that while the development of the embryo only takes 28 days, the young are likely to be born some 39–76 days after mating took place. The young remain with their mother for several weeks, gaining independence at about 10 weeks of age.

Muntjac
Muntiacus reevesi

This is the species of deer that you are most likely to encounter in Breckland, and it is often to be seen feeding alongside the roads through Thetford Forest. This introduced deer has continued to increase in both population size and distribution, its presence contributing to the loss of woodland flora and resulting in conservation challenges.

Description: A small and compact deer, about the size of a large dog but noticeably stocky in its hunched appearance. The arched posture, with head held low when foraging, is reminiscent of a pig. The male (known as a 'buck') has short and simple antlers, up to 10 cm or so in length; these are absent in the female (the 'doe'). The antlers, which grow through the summer, are shed in April or May. Males also have protruding canines, which curve backward; however, these are rarely as visible as those of a male Chinese Water Deer.

Both sexes show a well-marked facial pattern, with two darker stripes that run down the face to form a 'V'-shape that joins between the eyes (see photograph). Although sometimes approachable, individuals are easily spooked and may be seen running away with their tail erect. This reveals the white underside to the tail; the rump and top of the tail being dark chestnut brown in colour. Muntjac have a loud, abrupt barking call that may be heard throughout the year.

Similar species: Chinese Water Deer is the main confusion species, though this very slightly larger deer is rare in Breckland (with just a handful of records). Chinese Water Deer adopts a less-hunched posture and has larger more rounded ears; when seen head on, the ears, small dark eyes and shape of the muzzle are reminiscent of wallaby.

Where to look: Muntjac can be found throughout Thetford Forest and may be seen at Brandon Country Park and many other sites. They may also be encountered in suburban gardens and parks around Brandon and Thetford, including in the grounds of the BTO headquarters by Nun's Bridges, Thetford.

Behaviour: Although regarded as being secretive in habits, some of Breckland's Muntjac can be remarkably tolerant of human observers. Individuals favour thick undergrowth but regularly move into more open areas, including larger gardens, to feed. The presence of these deer may first be revealed by the small piles of shiny black droppings, roughly a centimetre in diameter and rounded in shape, that can be left on lawns overnight.

Muntjac are regular victims of collisions with motor traffic and populations are also controlled in order to reduce the damage caused to vulnerable woodland ecosystems. Muntjac densities within Breckland are some of the highest in Britain, reflecting the patterns of introduction and the availability of suitable habitat.

MAMMALS

Chinese Water Deer
Hydropotes inermis

The presence of this species in the Brecks probably has its origins in the escape of individuals from the former wildlife park at Kilverstone, just on the eastern edge of Thetford. Numbers are probably very low, and the species does not seem to have established itself here in quite the same way as it has in the Broads.

Description: Slightly larger than a Muntjac, the Chinese Water Deer has a compact body shape, with large rounded ears and black beady eyes. While some observers suggest that this species has a 'teddy bear'-like appearance, the large ears perhaps suggest wallaby rather than teddy bear. Neither sex has antlers. During the mating period (known as the 'rut') the males may give out a squeaking call. At other times, individuals produce a growling bark, longer in duration than that uttered by Muntjac.

Similar species: In addition to the features outlined under the 'Similar species' section within the Muntjac account, Chinese Water Deer has a shorter tail which is never held erect. Its stance and movement is more reminiscent of Roe Deer than of Muntjac; unlike Roe, it lacks the white rump patch.

Where to look: Although occasionally encountered on farmland, it is usually to be found in wetland areas, dominated by marsh and reedbed. Individuals have been recorded in the river valley fens of the Waveney Valley, including those of Redgrave and Lopham Fen. The species may also be seen at the RSPB's Lakenheath Fen reserve on the western edge of Breckland. Individuals are most active around dawn and dusk. Rather than bolting for cover, individuals will often stand and stare back at a human observer before moving off.

Behaviour: Chinese Water Deer were first introduced to Britain as residents of London Zoo in the 1870s. They were soon introduced to other collections, including Woburn and Whipsnade, and reports of escaped individuals in the wild started to emerge during the 1950s. The first Norfolk record appears to be 1968 and the first Suffolk record 1987.

Although generally solitary in habits, loose groups of individuals (typically females and their young) may be seen during early autumn. Adult males are territorial throughout the year and rut during December, when clashes between individuals may result in injury – the protruding canines being used as a weapon.

The British population probably only numbers a few thousand individuals, largely centred on the Norfolk Broads and the Cambridgeshire Fens. The species has not shown the rapid expansion in range evident with Muntjac, perhaps reflecting the more exacting habitat preferences of Chinese Water Deer. We are likely to see an increase in records from Breckland.

Red Deer
Cervus elaphus

This is the largest of our deer species, and one whose presence within Breckland can be traced back to Neolithic times thanks to archaeological finds at sites such as Grime's Graves, near Brandon. Predominantly associated with the plantations of Thetford Forest, individuals may sometimes be encountered on the surrounding heathland and farmland.

Description: This large deer, typically standing a metre tall at the shoulder, has a red-brown coat that (in the adult) lacks any white spotting. Males and females differ somewhat in appearance, the males being thickset with a shaggy neck and the females slimmer and slightly smaller. Adult males carry antlers, which are shed annually between March and April. The size of the antlers is related to the age of the male, with older males sporting larger antlers with more points.

Red Deer make use of wallows, particularly during the summer months when the coat is being replaced, and stags may also thrash vegetation during the autumn months (both to remove velvet and later as a form of display). Tracks, which may be found in soft ground, are larger than those of our other deer species, typically being 8–9 cm long and 6–7 cm wide in stags (smaller in hinds).

Similar species: Has a creamy-coloured rump and a brown unmarked tail, a feature useful where there is the potential for confusion with Fallow Deer (white rump, edged in black and bisected by black tail) and Sika Deer (rounded white rump, edged with brown, partially bisected by short black tail). Body size and antler characteristics (stags) are also useful features. Note that Sika Deer is not

currently known from Breckland, though has been recorded from elsewhere in Norfolk. The greatest risk of confusion is therefore with dark-coated Fallow Deer, individuals of which may sometimes fail to show the characteristic white spotting of this species.

Where to look: Red Deer hinds tend to be encountered more commonly than stags, the two sexes living separately for much of the year. Thetford Forest, particularly the blocks to the north of Thetford, are worth investigating, with small groups encountered fairly regularly by observers visiting the forest at dawn or dusk. During the rutting period, which runs from October to the end of November, stags may be heard roaring, the sound easily carrying over distances of a kilometre or more. Larger herds of females may sometimes be seen outside the forest, resting or feeding on the surrounding farmland. The fields to the east of Kilverstone (eastern edge of Thetford) have proved productive over recent years, as have those out on the Diss road towards Rushford, and in the area north of Cranwich.

Behaviour: Although particularly active around dawn and dusk, Red Deer may be encountered at any time of day, or indeed at any time of year. The two sexes form single-sex groups for much of the year, the males leaving their groups as the autumn rut approaches and moving to traditional rutting stands that are used from one year to the next. Young males tend to be more mobile than other individuals, wandering over a significant area.

The young (known as 'calves' and usually born singly) appear from late May to July, the hind having first chased away her calf from the previous year. Although the new calf will be left alone initially (except for feeding visits), it joins its mother after 1–2 weeks and may then become part of a larger crèche. The calves have a spotted coat when born but the spots are then lost when the calf undergoes its first moult at around two months of age. The British population of Red Deer is thought to number 350,000 individuals and has been increasing in some regions.

Adam Jones / BTO

Fallow Deer
Dama dama

The presence of Fallow Deer within Breckland is the result of introductions by the Normans and later landowners, who saw this species as either sporting quarry or as an ornamental additional to country estates. Escapes from deer parks have enabled it to become established more widely across the area, with movements into Thetford Forest the result of escapes from estates like Livermere Park and Ickworth Park.

Description: A large deer, intermediate in size between Roe and Red, and standing c.80–90 cm at the shoulder. This is the only British deer with palmate antlers – in which the angles between the points are partly filled to form a broad flat surface. The typical form (picture here) has a warm reddish-brown coat marked with white spots, but other colour forms do occur; these include dark brown, black, and white individuals. The antlers, which are palmate in adult males but spiked in young males, are shed in April and regrown again over the summer months. Rutting males may make similar calls to those made by Red Deer, but which are less drawn out and less far-carrying. Fallow prints are typically 6–7 cm long and 4 cm wide.

Similar species: See Red Deer (pages 68–69) for comparison with that species. The most likely confusion species is Sika Deer, a species currently absent from the Brecks. Perhaps the most useful feature on a Fallow Deer is the white rump, edged in black and bisected by the black line that runs from the back and down the length of the Fallow Deer tail. Roe is a smaller animal (60–75 cm at the shoulder) with a uniform coat colour and a black muzzle and matching moustachial marks. Roe has a cream-coloured rump, which lacks any obvious tail.

MAMMALS

Where to look: Uses both woodland and farmland habitats, often resting within the former and foraging within the latter. Mainly active at dawn and dusk and spends much of the day in cover. Within Breckland, and away from deer parks, they are most likely to be encountered in the southern part of Thetford Forest (known as 'King's Forest'), but they may also be encountered in the blocks to the north-west of Thetford, around Thetford Warren Lodge.

Behaviour: Fallow Deer are non-territorial in their habits and the foraging ranges of individual groups may overlap. Aggregations of several dozen individuals (many more in the case of populations living within deer parks) may form, though the stability of such groups tends to decline with group size. Research demonstrates that male groups are less stable than female-dominated groups.

This is a grazing species, for which grasses make up the bulk of the diet. In order to cope with this poor quality diet, Fallow Deer spend significant time ruminating to digest the material that they have eaten. During the autumn months they also take beech mast, acorns and seeds, to which may be added quantities of Ivy, bramble and Holly.

The rut takes place from October into November and sees males attempt to attract females through calling and display. Successful males mate with multiple females, resulting in the females each giving birth to a single fawn the following spring (either May or early June). Left in cover initially, the fawn is able to join its mother after 1–2 weeks, remaining with her for at least the next eight months. As with other deer, if you find an unaccompanied fawn, keep well away and leave it alone.

Populations away from deer parks probably number in excess of 125,000 individuals nationally, the species being most abundant in the south-east of England. Although less commonly encountered in Breckland than either Roe or Muntjac (and probably less than Red Deer), the Breckland population is important in a wider East Anglian context.

Roger Tidman / Nature Photographers

Roe Deer
Capreolus capreolus

Along with the much larger Red Deer, this is one of two deer species native to Britain. Favouring mixed landscapes that combine woodland cover and nearby fields, the Roe Deer is well distributed throughout Breckland. Despite this, it is less commonly encountered than the introduced Muntjac.

Description: A medium-sized deer, standing 60–75 cm at the shoulder. The body is short and compact, sitting on long legs and with a long neck. There is no obvious tail, leaving the rump patch exposed. This is rounded in the female (sometimes shaped like an upside-down heart) and kidney-shaped in the male. The face has an obvious black nose and a white chin (compare with Muntjac). Males carry simple antlers, set close together on the head; these are strongly ridged at their base, each up to 30 cm tall and ended with three tines ('points') in adults. Individuals may make a loud dog-like bark when flushed. Roe Deer tracks are small, being 4–5 cm in length and 3–4 cm across. Youngsters have white spots on their coat up until the time of their first moult.

Similar species: The plain coat and lack of any darker markings around the white rump patch enable separation from Fallow and Sika Deer. Size, posture and facial pattern allow separation from Muntjac and Chinese Water Deer. See the other species for more details.

Where to look: Although Roe Deer may be encountered throughout the Brecks, some of the best opportunities to view them come from within Thetford Forest. Individuals may be seen on forest rides at dawn and dusk and also viewed feeding

MAMMALS

on areas of clearfell, where the vegetation has been allowed to regrow. Others may be seen feeding on farmland, especially where this is located adjacent to suitable woodland habitat. Individuals are regularly seen from trains making the journey from Brandon to Ely, particularly during the autumn and winter months.

Behaviour: During the summer months Roe Deer are usually encountered singly or in small groups, the latter often involving several females and their young, perhaps accompanied by a male. Larger groups may form during the winter, but these either tend to be less stable affairs or involve a loose association of animals making use of the same feeding area. Males are territorial for part of the year, defending territories from March to September. These may be retained by the same individuals from one year to the next and are used during the rutting period (mid-July to the end of August), which is somewhat earlier than with other species of deer.

Activity is centred around dawn and dusk, but can occur throughout the 24-hour cycle. The amount of time spent feeding is linked to food availability and weather conditions, with more time spent foraging during the winter months than during the summer. Roe Deer are opportunistic when it comes to diet, taking a wide range of plant material depending on availability. The buds, leaves and shoots of deciduous trees are favoured, with an autumn switch to seeds and acorns, mushrooms and fruit. Agricultural crops, such as cereals, are often taken where available, sometimes in preference to other foods. This can bring Roe Deer into conflict with landowners.

Data from the BTO/JNCC/RSPB Breeding Bird Survey, whose volunteers also monitor common mammal species, show that the Roe Deer population increased by 86% between 1996 and 2016, though any change in abundance within East Anglia has been less apparent. The British population is currently thought to number in excess of 250,000 individuals.

Sarah Kelman / BTO

Watching Breckland's reptiles

Reptiles can be elusive, as they spend much of their time hidden away within vegetation or underground. They do bask, though, to raise their body temperatures, and chance sightings of basking or other activity are worth noting. With some knowledge of favoured habitats and reptile behaviour it is possible to catch up with them and to secure great views on a more predictable basis.

Stealth and caution are the watch words of the reptile watcher, since noise or vibration is often enough to drive them back into cover. Early spring, just after reptiles have emerged from hibernation, is the best time to seek them out. At this time of the year our reptiles spend significant amounts of time basking in sun, attempting to lift their body temperature. Snakes in particular tend to be more sluggish when doing this, providing the careful observer with an opportunity to approach and either watch or take photographs. Look for 'hotspot' patches of sunlight that are situated close to or within thicker cover; some of these will be located on south-facing slopes, while others might fall on bare ground within a patch of heather or other vegetation.

Thermoregulation is an important component of reptile behaviour and individuals may also make use of pieces of corrugated tin, old carpet or other debris, underneath which they can bask without attracting the attention of potential predators. By carefully lifting such items it is sometimes possible to spot Slow Worms and Grass Snakes, often in good numbers.

Our reptile species should not be picked up and handled. There is the risk of being bitten by Adder – which is venomous – and handling may damage the animal. This is a particular risk in the case of Slow Worm and Common Lizard, both of which may shed their tail as a form of anti-predator response. A pair of close-focusing binoculars can be very useful, providing you with an opportunity to watch from several metres distance but still enjoy excellent views of these creatures and their fascinating behaviour.

Why should you record what you see?

As noted on Page 5, records of a species at a location on a particular date provide the backbone of our knowledge, delivering information that can be used to protect

Adder, by Amy Lewis / BTO

REPTILES

species and the sites that they use. This is particularly important for reptiles, as many of their populations are threatened by habitat change and the loss of traditional sites.

Who should you send records to?
In addition to the Norfolk Biodiversity Information Service (NBIS) and Suffolk Biodiversity Information Service (SBIS) – the Local Environmental Records Centres (LERC) covering the Brecks and the central point for all records in their respective counties – you may also send your records direct to the relevant County Recorder, who verifies the records NBIS and SBIS receive. Information on who these people are can be found on the Norfolk and Norwich Naturalists' Society (NNNS) and the Suffolk Naturalists' Society (SNS) websites. If you are recording in more than one part of the country you could record on one platform, the most popular of which is iRecord (website and app).

Getting involved in monitoring and surveys
If you are reasonably competent at recording reptiles and/or wish to volunteer more regularly, you can take part in many monitoring or survey projects. The Amphibian and Reptile Conservation Trust (www.arc-trust.org) is the national organisation leading much of the work on reptiles and amphibians, running periodic surveys and ongoing monitoring programmes. The organisation also provides practical advice on things you can do to make your garden more reptile- and amphibian-friendly.

Another national organisation dedicated to the conservation of reptiles and amphibians is Froglife (www.froglife.org), which also provides advice and runs survey and monitoring projects. Froglife is a partner in Garden Wildlife Health (www.gardenwildlifehealth.org), through which reptile and amphibian disease is being monitored within garden habitats. One of the diseases being studied by the project is Snake Fungal Disease, which has only recently been discovered in the UK in Grass Snakes.

In addition to these national organisations, there are various local amphibian and reptile groups, coordinated through an umbrella organisation (www.arguk.org). Both Norfolk and Suffolk have active local groups.

Common Lizard, by Amy Lewis / BTO

Slow Worm
Anguis fragilis

This is the species of reptile most likely to be encountered in a garden setting within Breckland, reflecting the broad range of habitats that may be used. It is one of just two species of lizards found in the area and the only one lacking legs. Observers unfamiliar with Slow Worm may be alarmed by the superficial similarity to a snake, though this species is completely harmless.

Description: While there can be a degree of variation in background colour, all Slow Worms have a plain, smooth and shiny appearance, a feature that can also help separation from the two species of snakes that also occur in the Brecks. Adult males tend to be more uniform in colour than females, being grey or grey-brown; females are usually darker on their flanks and undersides and lighter on top. Their colour can vary from deep copper to golden brown. Some individuals (typically females) have subtle markings along the middle of their back, a feature that is also present in newly hatched youngsters (see photograph on opposite page). Occasional individuals may be found that are entirely black or which (usually males) have tiny blue markings across their body.

Young Slow Worms, which are live born by their mother, are small in size (c. 8 cm in length) and narrow in outline. Adults can reach 40 cm in length. Some individuals may lose the tips of their tail (see Behaviour) and end up with a more stubby appearance.

Similar species: Unlike snakes, Slow Worms have eyelids and a broad, flattened tongue. The lack of strong markings (though see earlier note about young Slow Worms) is another useful feature, as is the shiny appearance and body shape.

REPTILES

Where to look: Occupies a broad range of habitats, from rough grassland, heathland, coastal grasslands and open woodland to gardens, allotments and urban brownfield sites. Because of this they occur right across Breckland, though they are easily overlooked. One reason for this is that they tend not to bask out in the open, preferring to do so either under a suitable refuge (such as an old tin sheet) or in small patches of sunlight located within thicker cover. Individuals probably spend a great deal of time underground, again reducing the opportunity for the casual observer to chance across one. It is worth turning over old pieces of tin and other objects that might provide a suitable refuge; in fact, this method has been adopted by those seeking to discover whether Slow Worms are present at a site. Good numbers of Slow Worms may be seen at the BTO Nunnery Lakes Reserve (Thetford), where tin sheets have been put down for precisely this purpose.

Behaviour: In common with other lizards, Slow Worms are able to shed their tail when threatened by a potential predator. They are able to do this because of the 'fracture planes' present in some of the lower vertebrae. If attacked, the lizard can tighten muscles that cause the fracture to come apart, resulting in the loss of part of the tail. The severed tail will continue to thrash wildly for a few minutes, hopefully with the predator's interest taken up with this, rather than by the lizard making its escape.

Slow Worms emerge from hibernation during March, the males emerging before the females, and spend the initial days basking. Activity peaks during May and June – the best time to go out in search of these legless lizards – and it may also be influenced by the weather conditions. If it is particularly hot and dry then Slow Worms retreat underground. Adult females probably breed every other year, the young being produced during August and September. With the right conditions, Slow Worms do very well and form significant colonies. More information is needed on their distribution in Breckland, so do send your records in to your local county recorder.

Laurie Campbell / Nature Photographers Ltd

Common Lizard
Zootoca vivipara

This small lizard favours dry, open habitats and may sometimes be seen sunning itself on a bank, piece of wood or on open ground. They are, however, nervous creatures and quickly retreat into cover if they become aware of your presence. This is the only species of 'legged'-lizard to occur in Breckland.

Description: Typically 13–15 cm in length (including tail) and can be variable in terms of both its colour and in the strength of its body markings. Most individuals are tan-coloured in appearance, with a darker stripe down the middle of their back and with one or more paler stripes on their flanks.

Females tend to have darker flanks than males and are usually noticeably plumper in their appearance – particularly so when they are carrying eggs (see Behaviour). The long tail may sometimes be shortened through the loss of its tip (see Slow Worm). The young are dark-coloured at birth, but take on a coppery colour as they approach the end of the year and hibernation.

Similar species: The Sand Lizard does not occur in the Brecks, so it is important to be aware that Common Lizards can sometimes have a greenish tinge to their background colour. Some very green individuals are known from other parts of the country. Newts, which have a terrestrial phase to their annual cycle, are superficially similar in their appearance but unlike lizards they do not have scales on their skin. Common Lizards may sometimes enter water and swim.

Where to look: Heathland, open woodland and other open habitats are favoured and the species is best searched for at heathland sites such as Thetford Warren Lodge, Knettishall Heath, West Stow Country Park and Cavenham Heath. Best seen

REPTILES

when basking in the sun, behaviour that is most likely to be encountered early in the spring (March to May), or early in the morning when lower temperatures force these reptiles to spend longer warming up. Basking is also important during the autumn, before the lizards enter hibernation.

One of the best ways to find Common Lizards is to move slowly and quietly along the narrow paths that often criss-cross areas of heathland. Scan the sunny patches on nearby banks and, in particular, seek out sheltered spots where the sunlight falls onto a fallen branch or other piece of wood; such sites are often favoured by basking lizards.

Behaviour: This species is sometimes referred to as the Viviparous Lizard, a reference to the live young that are delivered by the female, as opposed to the young hatching from eggs. In actual fact the young are born with their transparent egg membrane still attached, something from which they quickly emerge. Pregnant females spend longer periods basking than other individuals and may be recognised by their plump appearance.

Basking behaviour underlines that lizards and other reptiles are limited by temperature. Interestingly, the Common Lizard is better adapted to the cold than virtually any other reptile, and this is one reason why its UK population extends to the north of Scotland. Individuals do, however, retreat to winter refuges from October onwards, entering hibernation and remaining there until the following spring. Hibernation in this species is not just important for overwinter survival; females will not breed successfully the following year unless they have been exposed to winter cold and the associated hibernation.

Populations appear to live in loose colonies, suggesting that favourable local conditions can support good numbers of individuals. These lizards feed on a range of different invertebrates, from earthworms and small snails, through to beetles, bugs and larger insects.

Mike Toms / BTO

Adder
Vipera berus

Breckland's forests and heathlands are home to Britain's only venomous snake, the Adder. Although widely distributed in suitable habitats across the area, populations at many sites have declined, the species suffering from habitat change and, in some locations, persecution.

Description: Best identified by the strong zig-zag markings along its back, and the 'v'-shaped mark at the back of the head. Individuals may vary in colour from silvery-white through to black, via various browns. Males are usually silvery-white in their background colour and have dark brown or black markings. Females tend to be light brown or warm brown in background colour, with darker brown markings. All-black individuals are not uncommon in some populations.

A fairly small and somewhat stocky snake, averaging 50 cm in length in males and 55 cm in females. Although there are records of individuals reaching up to 90 cm in length, Adders rarely reach 65 cm or more.

Similar species: Should be fairly straightforward to distinguish from Grass Snake and Slow Worm. The more similar Smooth Snake does not occur in the area.

Where to look: Adults are easiest to find and watch early in the year, when they first emerge from hibernation (March to April). Adders spend more of their time basking than our other snakes and favour the middle of the day for this behaviour over early morning or late afternoon. A sheltered spot on a sunny bank, or in an open hollow within stands of heather, may be used over several days, the snake adjusting its location in response to the weather conditions.

REPTILES

These early season basking sites are, at least in the case of the males, located close to where individuals spent the winter. Later in the season the snakes tend to be dispersed over larger areas. Once learnt, knowledge of local hibernation sites can enable human observers to secure good views of the snakes. For a more casual observer, lacking local knowledge, the best approach is to visit suitable sites, such as Thetford Warren Lodge, Knettishall Heath, Cavenham Heath and clearfell blocks within Thetford Forest. By moving slowly and scanning the ground ahead of you, it should be possible to approach a basking snake to within a few metres. Adders are best viewed with binoculars, so as not to disturb them.

Behaviour: Adders have a well-developed pattern of thermoregulation, and use the sun's warmth to maintain a body temperature of around 33°C. During the cold winter months the snakes retreat underground, seeking out suitable frost-free sites, many of which may be used by several individuals. The first snakes emerge during late February or early March, depending upon the conditions. They may then spend several weeks basking, flattening their bodies (see photograph opposite) to maximise the amount of their body exposed to the sun.

Males seek out reproductively active females, travelling up to 200 metres a day in their search for a suitable mate. If a courting male encounters another male then the two may engage in combat, with each individual trying to gain the upper position and to push his opponent to the ground. This can result in the 'dancing Adders' described in some literature. The result of a successful mating will be the live young that are born in late August or early September. These young snakes, which are just 14–18 cm in length, soon enter hibernation and have to rely on their yolk sac for nutrients, since they will not feed until they emerge from hibernation the following year.

Adders continue to be persecuted because people are fearful of them and their venom. Populations have declined in many areas, with habitat loss an additional problem for this interesting and beautiful reptile.

Mike Toms / BTO

Grass Snake
Natrix natrix

A large snake, with a distinctive yellow collar, olive-green body and a pattern of faint black markings. Most often found in damp habitats located close to water, the Grass Snake may also visit larger rural gardens, where it sometimes lays its eggs in the warmth of a garden compost heap.

Description: While the largest individuals may reach 1.5 m in length, most are considerably smaller (typically 70 to 90 cm in length). The background colour is a dull olive-green, with two black crescent-shaped markings sitting behind a pale yellow neck band. The pale colouring extends along the bottom of the head, broken by a series of vertical black stripes. Further black markings extend along the flanks, with additional but less obvious black spotting evident along the back. Young Grass Snakes, newly emerged from their eggs, show similar markings but are often darker in their appearance; they are about the thickness and length of a pencil.

Similar species: Unlikely to be confused with Adder or Slow Worm.

Where to look: As its name suggests, most commonly associated with damp grassland habitats, often situated close to bodies of water, such as ponds and rivers. It may also make use of drier sites, particularly if these provide suitable ground cover. Larger gardens, also with available ground cover, may be used if the levels of disturbance are low. Here the snakes often congregate around compost heaps, basking on the surface or under any covering fabric, and laying their eggs within the heap itself. The species, which is found throughout Breckland, is most likely to be encountered in the river valley fens. In addition to sites like Redgrave and Lopham Fen, it is regularly encountered on the BTO Nunnery Lakes Reserve

to the south of Thetford, where individuals make good use of the reptile tiles distributed around the site. Other good sites are Foulden Common (near Foulden village), West Stow Country Park and the old gravel pits at Lynford.

Behaviour: Specialises in amphibians, taking both Common Frogs and Common Toads; it will also feed on fish and small mammals. Young Grass Snakes feed on insects and slugs. Lacking venom, the prey is caught and swallowed alive, the backwards facing teeth helping the snake to swallow what it has caught. If disturbed, a Grass Snake may produce a foul-smelling substance from its stomach; it may also pretend to be dead. Unsurprisingly, given their preferred diet, Grass Snakes are excellent swimmers and are often seen in the water, where their 'S'-shaped swimming motion carries them with ease. The head is held above the water's surface when swimming in this way, while the rest of the body tends to be just below the surface.

Emergence from hibernation usually occurs in March and early April, the snakes initially spending several days basking before moving away from the locality of their wintering site. Egg-laying takes place in June or July, with each female laying up to 40 soft-shelled eggs under decaying vegetation – which is why compost heaps prove so attractive to them. The first young will emerge in August, with others following in September. Just a few weeks later and the snakes enter hibernation (from October).

Populations have almost certainly benefited from the growing trend for more wildlife-friendly approaches to gardening. However, many individuals are probably killed by domestic Cats, lawn mowers and strimmers. Others may be deliberately killed by people, fearful that they might be Adders. Changes in the wider countryside, particularly the loss of so many ponds and wet meadows, has probably left today's Grass Snake population at a much lower level than was present just a few decades ago.

Watching Breckland's amphibians

Because our amphibians mate and reproduce in water they are tied to ponds and other waterbodies for part of the year, making them easier to catch up with than is the case with reptiles. Knowledge of emergence patterns and the timing of breeding, coupled with an understanding of how weather conditions may influence both of these processes, can enable you to target sites at just the right time. For example, knowing that mild damp nights in early March can prompt Common Toad migration can help you plan visits to breeding ponds to watch arrivals.

Although amphibians are generally more approachable than reptiles, they are often hidden out of sight or may disappear into cover or dive to the depths of a pond if disturbed. Common Frogs are more wary than many amphibians, but are more approachable when they gather in their mating aggregations or when they are chanced upon on land. Newts often hide within aquatic vegetation when disturbed, but by sitting still it should be possible to watch them, especially during the warmer summer months when they need to take air at the water's surface.

Our amphibians tend to be more active at night than during the day. One of the best ways to see newts is to search ponds by torchlight on warm evenings after dark during April or May. Provided the water is clear and not completely obscured by vegetation, newts that were invisible during the day can be found. During their terrestrial phase many amphibians seek shelter under piles of wood or stones, which can be lifted and replaced carefully in order to discover the species present.

While it may not always be possible to catch up with the adults, their presence at a site may be revealed through the eggs that have been deposited. Frog and toad spawn is characteristic, the former in clumps, the latter in strings. Frog spawn is readily found where it has been deposited, often in the warmer shallows, just breaking the water surface. Toad spawn can be harder to spot, as it lies below the surface, often trailed among vegetation. Newt eggs are laid singly, often with pond weed leaves folded around them.

Common Frog tadpole, by Sarah Kelman / BTO

AMPHIBIANS

Recording what you see and why it matters

As noted throughout this book, we badly need more information on the numbers and distribution of our amphibian species. Such information is essential if we are to monitor the success of conservation efforts or provide accurate information to support land management decisions. Such information is particularly important for amphibians, as many of their populations are threatened by habitat change and the loss of traditional breeding ponds.

In addition to the Norfolk Biodiversity Information Service (NBIS) and Suffolk Biodiversity Information Service (SBIS) – the Local Environmental Records Centres (LERC) covering the Brecks and the central point for all records in their respective counties – you may also send your records direct to the relevant County Recorder, who verifies the records NBIS and SBIS receive. Information on who these people are can be found on the Norfolk and Norwich Naturalists' Society (NNNS) and the Suffolk Naturalists' Society (SNS) websites.

Getting involved in monitoring and surveys

As noted in the section on Breckland's reptiles, there are plenty of opportunities to get involved in monitoring or survey projects. Details of the organisations working on amphibians are included on page 75, but do also look for other opportunities provided through Norfolk Wildlife Trust (www.norfolkwildlifetrust.org.uk) and Suffolk Wildlife Trust (www.suffolkwildlifetrust.org). These organisation also provide practical advice on things you can do to make your garden more amphibian-friendly. If you have a pond in your garden please do monitor it for amphibians. As well as submitting information on the species using the pond, records of when spawn first appears can be used in national projects, such as Nature's Calendar (www.naturescalendar.woodlandtrust.org.uk), charting the impacts of a changing climate. Amphibian diseases, of which several are known for Common Frogs, can also be monitored by watching your garden pond – see Garden Wildlife Health (www.gardenwildlifehealth.org) for more details.

Common Toad, by John Harding / BTO

Smooth Newt
Lissotriton vulgaris

Of the three native newts, this is the one most likely to be encountered in Breckland. It is also the UK's most widespread and abundant newt species, equally at home in garden ponds and larger waterbodies in the wider countryside. Individuals only spend a small part of the year in water, and for the rest of the time they lead a terrestrial existence.

Description: Reaching 10 cm in length, the Smooth Newt (sometimes referred to as the Common Newt) is the smaller of the two newt species likely to be encountered in the Brecks. Males are slightly larger than females. The upperparts are a dull olive-brown colour, marked with darker brown spots; these are larger and more pronounced in the adult male than female. The underparts are buff-coloured, with an orange-yellow central patch, and a pale throat which is spotted (see photographs).

During the breeding season the male Smooth Newt develops a wavy-edged crest, which extends from the shoulders along the back and down the length of the tail to its tip. During the terrestrial phase, the lack of crest and overall dull brown colour can give the appearance of a lizard. Smooth Newt eggs are laid singly, folded into the leaf of a plant. The larva that emerges from the egg is light brown in colour, with distinctive feathery gills and a rounded tail tip.

Similar species: Palmate Newt, which is rare or absent from Breckland, is similar in general appearance, but has a pale unspotted throat and a filamentous end to its tail, something that is particularly evident in adult males. Great Crested Newt has rough looking skin and tends to be darker in coloration; the male crest has a strongly ragged edge.

AMPHIBIANS

Where to look: Occurs in a wide range of waterbodies, but shows a preference for smaller, fish-free, ponds and ditches. Garden ponds, free from goldfish, may support good populations, as may some of the fire ponds maintained throughout Thetford Forest. More active at night than during the day, individuals may also be easier to see at dawn and dusk. Activity at breeding ponds occurs from March to June, so time visits to suitable sites to April or May. Damp evenings during this period can encourage overland movement of Smooth Newts back to their breeding ponds, making torch-lit searches worthwhile. Individuals may be found at other times of the year by careful searching under logs and larger stones located close to ponds.

Behaviour: Adults do not develop their breeding characteristics until they have returned to their breeding ponds in spring. Once the males attain their crest they will attempt to attract a mate with a series of complex and well-studied courtship displays. Growing a crest is energetically costly, and males with larger crests are more likely to secure a mate.

Once mated, the female will produce and lay up to 300 eggs, each of which is deposited singly, wrapped in the leaf of a water plant. Depending on the water temperature, the eggs will hatch within 2–3 weeks, the resulting larvae spending their first few weeks of life well hidden within aquatic vegetation. Some will metamorphose into their adult form before the end of the year, but others will remain in the pond to overwinter as larvae.

Smooth Newts have many predators, and mortality rates of larvae are particularly high. Some will fall victim to dragonfly nymphs, while others will be taken by fish – hence the preference for fish-free ponds – or by Water Shrews. Adults may even fall victim to Blackbirds, some of which have learnt how to grab the newts from the shallows of garden ponds. While some newt populations have probably benefited from the creation of garden ponds, others will have lost out to the vast numbers of farmland ponds filled in over the last few decades.

Moss Taylor / BTO

Great Crested Newt
Triturus cristatus

The Great Crested Newt is a more strongly aquatic species than its smaller relatives. Declines in its populations have seen the species given special legal protection and it is an offence under the Wildlife & Countryside Act 1981 to disturb Great Crested Newts or to damage the ponds and other sites at which they occur. The species is sometimes referred to as the 'warty newt', reflecting its rough skin.

Description: This is the largest of the three British newts, the females (which are slightly larger on average than the males) reaching up to 16 cm in length. The most obvious feature is the rough 'warty' skin, usually dark in colour though speckled with white dots along the side. During the breeding season the adult males develop a large, ragged-edged crest. The throat is dark, again with white speckling, and the underside is bright orange, with large dark blotches. Great Crested Newt eggs are (at 5 mm) about twice the size of those produced by either of our smaller native newt species, while the resulting larvae are dark in coloration and have a deep and pointed tail. Despite their larger size, Great Crested Newt larvae can be difficult to distinguish from those of other newt species.

Similar species: The rough appearance of the skin, coupled with the white speckling and dark throat should allow separation from both Smooth Newt and Palmate Newt. Non-native populations of Italian Crested Newt have become established in some parts of the UK, but fortunately are not known from Breckland.

Where to look: As noted above, this species has been given special legal protection and should not be disturbed without a licence. It appears to favour larger and deeper waterbodies than those used by our other newt species, but it

AMPHIBIANS

can sometimes be found using small ponds, especially where several occur within a small area. Adults can enter breeding ponds as early as January, with most leaving these again during July. During the terrestrial phase they may be found at some distance from water, seeking shelter under logs, stones and other features. Records of the species come from across Breckland, with particular concentrations within the Stamford Army Training Area and the northern parts of Thetford Forest.

Behaviour: Both more nocturnal than our other newts and more likely to spend time at the bottom of favoured waterbodies than utilise the upper layers. This may make them less vulnerable to certain predators. Adults have to breathe air, so they are forced to make regular forays to the water's surface to take a gulp of air before retreating back to the bottom.

Display forms a central role within courtship, the males often gathering within a particular part of a pond for this purpose. Display is used both to attract a mate and to intimidate other males. Courtship and egg-laying can begin very early in the year if the winter has been mild, with the first eggs being deposited as early as February – though March is more usual. Great Crested Newts first breed when they are 2–4 years of age; they are relatively long-lived, with an average life expectancy of 7–8 years.

Once the eggs hatch, the resulting larvae often swim freely within the water column, rather than remaining hidden within aquatic vegetation. This behaviour probably makes them more vulnerable to fish predation and may explain the avoidance of ponds containing fish, evident in this species. Fully grown larvae are 6–7 cm in length, making them as large as many adult Smooth Newts. The young newts leave the pond following metamorphosis, though many return later in the season, presumably to exploit the feeding opportunities on offer. The young newts have toxins in their skin, which may confer some defence against predators. The newts seek out terrestrial hiding places from October, using these to overwinter and to sit out the challenging conditions.

Paul Sterry / Nature Photographers

Common Toad
Bufo bufo

Common Toads only enter water for a short period during the spring, when they can gather together in large numbers to breed; throughout the rest of the year they live a terrestrial existence and may be encountered some distance from the nearest water.

Description: The rough looking, warty skin is a distinctive feature. The 'warts' contain a toxin that may be secreted when the toad is threatened by a predator. Secretion of the toxin is used as a last resort however, the toad giving plenty of warning by inflating its body and raising itself up on its legs. Note the characteristic iris shape, and how this differs from that of Common Frog. Colour may vary from a warm ochre through to a dull olive-grey.

Adult females may reach 90 mm in length, while the males are somewhat smaller and typically only reach 70 mm. Tadpoles are black in colour and lack the spotting present on the tadpoles of Common Frog. If in doubt, look at the tip of the tail, which is pointed in Common Frog and round in Common Toad.

Similar species: Natterjack Toad is a rare species, whose Norfolk and Suffolk populations are restricted to a small number of sites around the coast.

Where to look: Although individual toads may be found in many of Breckland's gardens, it is the larger breeding aggregations that tend to catch the attention of those interested in the species. Such groups tend to be focused on larger ponds, lakes and flooded gravel pits, where many thousands of individual toads may congregate. Within the Brecks there are a number of sites where Toadwatch and/or Froglife volunteers work to minimise the number of toads killed crossing busy

roads on their way to traditional breeding ponds. These include Cranwich, Cockley Cley and Oxborough in Norfolk, and West Stow and Redgrave & Lopham Fen in Suffolk. Toad migration is heavily influenced by the weather conditions, with damp weather during March prompting movement towards the breeding ponds. During 2018, some 4,500 toads were reported from the crossing at Cranwich on the A134 between Mundford and Northwold, with in excess of 900 individuals recorded on each of two nights in the second week of March.

Behaviour: Toad migration usually takes place during the evening and numbers at favoured breeding sites continue to build over several days. Males invariably outnumber the larger females because they arrive earlier and remain at the pond for longer, resulting in stiff competition for a mate. Many of the females will arrive at the pond with a male already on their back – the male clasps the female in what is termed 'amplexus' – and other males then attempt to displace him to claim the female for themselves. Where there are large numbers of males in attendance a mating ball can develop, sometimes resulting in the female being killed through drowning. Spawning does not necessarily begin when the toads first arrive at the pond, and there is usually a delay of a couple of days before it appears. Toad spawn is deposited in strings, which are made up of double and alternating rows of black eggs. The strings are wrapped around vegetation and each may contain in excess of 1,000 eggs.

Toads appear able to exploit larger ponds that may be avoided by Common Frogs because of their fish populations; toad tadpoles contain similar toxins to the adults and so are distasteful to many predators. Although we lack data from structured national surveys, there is evidence to suggest that Common Toad populations have undergone a significant level of decline over recent decades. In addition to the toll taken when crossing busy roads, they may face other pressures, from the loss of breeding ponds to detrimental changes in habitat quality and availability, something that has triggered targeted conservation efforts.

Mike Toms / BTO

Common Frog
Rana temporaria

Probably our most familiar amphibian, occupying a broad range of habitats, from urban parks and gardens to areas of rough grassland and woodland. Individuals may be encountered throughout the Brecks, but are perhaps best viewed when they arrive at traditional spawning sites in spring.

Description: Although the background colour is usually some shade of brown or green, Common Frogs come in a variety of colours, with yellow or russet individuals sometimes encountered. On top of the background colour are darker markings, usually brown or black, which vary in both extent and intensity. These tend to be located on the head, back and legs. Most individuals show the dark patch behind the eye. Individual frogs have the ability to lighten or darken their background colour according to environmental conditions and it is interesting to note that breeding males tend to have a grey appearance.

Adult Common Frogs are 60–90 mm in body length, with males slightly smaller on average than females. Tadpoles, which can reach 35 mm in length, are brown in colour, with tiny gold- or brass-coloured spots. Spawn is laid in clumps that average 10–15 mm across.

Similar species: The rounded snout and more widely spaced eyes of Common Frog aid separation from the much rarer Pool Frog (see page 94) and other water frogs that may sometimes result from accidental introductions. The largely smooth and moist skin, coupled with eye colour, helps to distinguish Common Frog from our native toad species. The spawn is deposited in clumps, while that of toads is deposited in strings.

AMPHIBIANS

Where to look: A range of still waterbodies is used by breeding frogs, from a scatter of puddles through to large ponds; on rare occasions they may spawn in flowing water. They tend to avoid waterbodies that have established fish populations, but may sometimes occupy the shallow parts of these. Away from water, Common Frogs can be found in many habitats, though only where conditions are suitably damp since these frogs need to keep their skin moist. Small to medium-sized ponds in the Brecks, at sites such as Foulden Common, Thompson Common and Lynford, are worth visiting, particularly during early spring. Garden ponds are often well used also, and probably support important populations.

Behaviour: Males gather at favoured spawning sites from early spring, the females typically arriving a few days later. As more individuals arrive so the chorus of low-pitched croaking grows in volume and the site becomes a mass of frogs and spawn, with individuals jostling for position. Competition for access to the females can be fierce, with several males forming a mating 'ball' with a single female. A successful male will grasp the female with his front legs, locking them under her armpits and across her chest; a mating pair in this position is known as being in 'amplexus.' Each female may produce an egg mass containing up to 2,000 eggs, after which she leaves the breeding pond. The frogs disperse once breeding is over, but many remain in or close to the pond for the remainder of the year. Some individuals overwinter in terrestrial refugia, such as log piles and compost heaps, while others hibernate in the mud at the bottom of ponds.

The first froglets usually appear from midsummer, some 10–15 weeks after hatching, though development is influenced by temperature and food availability within the breeding pond. Mortality of tadpoles and froglets is high, with many lost to predatory fish and the larvae of water beetles and dragonflies. Adult frogs may suffer from various diseases, with cases of 'red leg' – which is caused by a bacterium – sometimes reported from frog populations inhabiting garden ponds.

Moss Taylor / BTO

Pool Frog
Pelophylax lessonae

The last native individuals of this species were lost from Breckland during the mid-1990s; with their disappearance the Pool Frog became extinct as a British species. More recently, thanks to the efforts of a collaborative programme led by Amphibian and Reptile Conservation and Natural England, the Pool Frog has been reintroduced to Norfolk Wildlife Trust's Thompson Common (its last UK site).

Description: Reintroduced Pool Frogs belong to the northern European race, which genetic studies show included the English individuals that were lost during the 1990s. These show less green on their backs and flanks than the southern race, individuals of which have been introduced to sites in southern England. Pool frogs have a prominent yellow or green dorsal stripe. In northern Pool Frogs the dorsal coloration of males is olive green, changing to a lime green at the peak of breeding. Females are dark brown, almost black in some cases, with contrasting marbled patterns on the flanks.

Similar species: Similar in size to Common Frog, but the markings readily distinguish the species; Common Frogs lack the Pool Frog's dorsal stripe and have a dark patch behind the eye. Separation from other 'water frogs', such as Edible Frog (which has a small introduced population in East Norfolk) is more difficult. Edible Frog is a non-native hybrid between Pool Frog and the non-native Marsh Frog. It tends to be more green in its appearance than northern race Pool Frog, and has greyish-white vocal sacs in the male, as opposed to white. Relative leg length is used to distinguish between the species, but the calls made during late spring and early summer are a more practical means of identifying water frogs in the field.

AMPHIBIANS

Where to look: The recent releases have been made to part of Thompson Common that is closed to public access, affording the frogs an opportunity to develop a new population without disturbance. As the population grows it is hoped that it will spread and recolonise ponds located within public areas. The species is afforded special protection under the Wildlife & Countryside Act 1981.

Behaviour: More aquatic in its habits than Common Frog, spending more of the year in or around suitable waterbodies. Individuals often sit at the water's surface among floating vegetation or bask on the bank; they appear to be more confiding and less nervous than Common Frog so can be approached more readily (assuming that you have an appropriate licence).

The frogs emerge from hibernation during late March or early April, but breeding does not occur until May or early June. During the mating season the male Pool Frogs advertise their presence with characteristic calls, reminiscent of a quacking duck. The females are attracted by the calling behaviour and, during mating, produce five or six small clumps of spawn with brown ova. After egg-laying the females retreat to the quieter parts of the pond.

Pool Frog tadpoles are smaller than those of Common Frog when they first emerge from the egg, but grow rapidly over the course of the summer. Eventually, they will be significantly larger in size than those of their more common relative. Their development is heavily weather dependent, with greater numbers of froglets emerging in warmer summers, appearing in ponds from late July.

The Pool Frogs that have been reintroduced to Thompson Common come from the Swedish population, which is genetically similar to that which disappeared from Breckland in the mid-1990s. The darker colour of these northern race individuals is thought to be driven by the thermoregulatory advantages that being darker brings at more northern latitudes.

Female Pool frog / John Baker

Index

Adder..80–81
American Mink...65
Badger..54–55
Bank Vole..8
Barbastelle..38–39
Brandt's Bat..42–43
Brown Hare...20–21
Brown Long-eared Bat.......................36–37
Chinese Water Deer..................................67
Common Frog....................................92–93
Common Lizard..................................78–79
Common Pipistrelle...........................46–47
Common Rat...17
Common Shrew..26
Common Toad....................................90–91
Daubenton's Bat................................40–41
Edible Dormouse..6
Fallow Deer...70–71
Ferret..64
Field Vole...9
Grass Snake..82–83
Great Crested Newt...........................88–89
Grey Squirrel...6–7
Harvest Mouse...................................12–13
Hedgehog...22–23
House Mouse..16
Leisler's Bat..32–33
Mole..24–25
Muntjac..4, 66
Nathusius' Pipistrelle.........................50–51
Natterer's Bat.....................................44–45
Noctule...30–31
Otter...56–57
Polecat..62–63
Pool Frog..94–95
Pygmy Shrew..27
Rabbit...18–19
Red Deer...68–69
Red Fox...52–53
Red Squirrel..7
Roe Deer...72–73
Serotine..34–35
Slow Worm...76–77
Smooth Newt.....................................86–87
Soprano Pipistrelle.............................48–49
Stoat...58–59
Water Shrew......................................28–29
Water Vole..10–11
Weasel..60–61
Whiskered Bat...................................42–43
Wood Mouse...14
Yellow-necked Mouse...............................15